Foolproof French \

Copyright © 2019-2020 by Allison Grant Lounes.

All rights reserved. No part of this publication may be reproduced, distributed, or transmitted in any form or by any means, including photocopying, recording, or other electronic or mechanical methods, without the prior written permission of the publisher, except in the case of brief quotations embodied in critical reviews and certain other noncommercial uses permitted by copyright law. For permission requests, write to the publisher at the address below.

Allison Grant Lounes
www.yourfranceformation.com
welcometo@yourfranceformation.com

Ordering Information:
Quantity sales. Special discounts are available on quantity purchases by corporations, associations, and others. For details, contact the author at the address above.

Foolproof French Visas Version Information

Because you need to have the most up-to-date information for your visa application, it is important to know when the most recent changes to French legislation regarding visas went into effect, and when the information contained in this book was most recently updated.

This Second Edition is completely up-to-date as of its publication date of **August 1, 2020** and contains information on procedures and legislation currently in effect. The most recent changes to the visa application process went into effect through October 2018 in the United States (visa applications though VFS Global in all US jurisdictions, and the ability to go to any VFS office). The most recent changes to legislation regarding visa types went into effect in **January 2020**. It includes some minor edits and clarifications, as well as an expanded Brexit section, as the Brexit rules were clarified in early 2020.

Please note that at the time of releasing the second edition, the French borders are currently closed to Americans and only student visa applications are being processed in about half of the VFS Global facilities. Other visa types are not being processed at all. Some préfectures in France have temporarily modified their procedures and have backlogged appointments. Please check your local préfecture's guidance for renewals prior to scheduling your appointment or submitting your renewal dossier. At this time, there is no evidence that these temporary changes in préfecture procedures will become permanent, and this edition of Foolproof French Visas cannot cover the individual procedures of each French department.

It is likely that France will open its borders progressively and begin processing certain categories of visa applications prior to opening up to general tourism. As of the publication of this edition, there are no significant permanent changes to the visa application procedures outside of France.

The first edition of Foolproof French visas was published on October 1, 2019.
The second edition was published on August 1, 2020.

Changes for Version 2:
- Clarified the "Working Remotely" Section
- Updated and expanded the "VLS-VTS" and "OFII Vignette" sections to reflect new online procedures and provide clarification.
- Added information on procedures for foreign children turning 18 in France
- Expanded the Brexit Section to include carte de séjour request procedures and add details about the procedurs for TCN spouses of British citizens.
- Updated cost of timbre fiscal for OFII procedures and renewals to reflect 2020 prices
- Updated au pair visa section regarding renewals

- Edited weird stuff in TAPIF section
- Updated required documents to remove background check (now done by VFS) and remove the now-defunct paper OFII form
- Updated Microentreprise income limits to reflect current figures
- Clarification of PACS procedures and visa options
- Added details about the visa for the non-French parent of a French child
- Added tips for making the VFS website work properly
- Clarified details about submitting your passport
- Moved information for after arrival into a new section
- Added section "The Visa Application Submission Process"
- Expanded information on applying for residency (a 10-year card) and naturalization
- Updated and expanded materials on clarifying your next steps
- Updated links and details about scheduling a consultation

Table of Contents

FOOLPROOF FRENCH VISAS VERSION INFORMATION	**2**
TABLE OF CONTENTS	**5**
INTRODUCTION	**8**
THE EVER-CHANGING REGULATIONS ON FRENCH VISAS	9
WHO (WHAT NATIONALITIES) IS THIS BOOK FOR?	10
SCHENGEN TRAVEL RULES	**13**
WHAT IS SCHENGEN?	13
APPLYING FOR A LONG-STAY VISA AFTER SCHENGEN TRAVEL	15
ARRIVING EARLY IN SCHENGEN	15
OVERSTAYING A LONG-STAY VISA	16
TRAVELING IN SCHENGEN AS A FRENCH RESIDENT	16
WORKING IN SCHENGEN AS A FRENCH RESIDENT	17
WORKING IN FRANCE WITH ANOTHER SCHENGEN COUNTRY'S VISA	18
WORKING REMOTELY	18
HELPFUL VOCABULARY	**22**
VISA, CARTE DE SÉJOUR, TITRE DE SÉJOUR	23
FRENCH CONSULATES & VFS GLOBAL	32
PRÉFECTURES & SOUS-PRÉFECTURES	34

COMPARING & EVALUATING LONG-STAY VISA TYPES 35

HEALTH INSURANCE 35
INCOME & SAVINGS REQUIREMENT 36
WORK 36
TAXATION 39
BRITISH CITIZENS REMAINING IN FRANCE AFTER BREXIT 43

NON-WORK VISAS 49

LONG SÉJOUR TEMPORAIRE 50
LONG-STAY VISITOR VISA 56

APPLYING FOR A FRENCH VISA 70

DOCUMENTS YOU MAY NEED 71
ACCOMPANYING FAMILY MEMBERS 77
USING THE FRANCE-VISAS WEBSITE 83
WHERE TO APPLY 86
MAKING AN APPOINTMENT 87
TIMELINE FOR APPLYING 89
THE VISA APPLICATION SUBMISSION PROCESS 92
COMMON REASONS FOR VISA REJECTIONS 96
REJECTIONS, NEW APPLICATIONS & APPEALS 103

ARRIVING IN FRANCE 105

1. FIND HOUSING. 106
2. PURCHASE A TIMBRE FISCAL DÉMATÉRIALISÉ. 107
3. COMPLETE THE ONLINE OFII FORM. 108
4. RECEIVE YOUR CONVOCATION(S). 108
5. GO TO YOUR OFII VISITS. 109
6. IF YOU MUST MISS AN OFII VISIT. 111
7. KEEP YOUR DOCUMENTATION. 112
8. SET A REMINDER TO RENEW YOUR VISA. 112
RENEWING YOUR VISA 113

FOOLPROOF FRENCH VISAS : RETIREMENT EDITION

CHANGING YOUR VISA STATUS IN FRANCE   125

GETTING HELP WITH YOUR VISA APPLICATION   131

FRANCEFORMATION CLIENT CASE STUDIES   152
DID YOU KNOW?   164
CLIENT TESTIMONIALS   165
SCHEDULE A CONSULTATION   169
ALSO BY ALLISON LOUNES   171

Introduction

If you want to move to France, you may not know where to begin in evaluating all of the different ways to move to France, establishing which visas you could potentially apply for, or which types of international mobility programs you may be eligible for.

This book is going to provide an overview of each type of visa so you can determine the visa type most compatible with your move and understand how to apply for it. For each visa type, we'll not only cover the requirements for obtaining each visa, but also what you are and are not allowed to do on each visa type. The goal is to not only help you to choose the visa that is most appropriate for your stay in France, but also to help you create a long-term plan for staying in France if you would like, and for helping you to understand the vocabulary and administrative procedures related to your stay.

By the end of this book you should:
- ✓ Understand the different vocabulary related to the visa application and renewal process.
- ✓ Know what visa type is most appropriate for you and what documents you will need to submit to apply for it.
- ✓ Know the timeline of when you should begin acquiring documents and when you want to arrive in France.

- ✓ Understand how to maintain and renew your selected visa type.
- ✓ Understand if you will ever have to change your visa status and whether or not you will become eligible for permanent residency in France (10-year carte de résident) or naturalization as a French citizen.
- ✓ Know what documents you need to submit for a visa application for yourself and your family members and how to maximize your chances for success.
- ✓ Understand what you will need to do to renew your visa at the end of your first year, and what documents you will be required to submit.

The Ever-Changing Regulations on French Visas

I have been in the business of helping people with French visas since I started writing Paris Unraveled in 2010, and began offering services to those moving to France in 2012. The different visa types, their regulations and requirements, and the procedures for applying and renewing have all changed, for each visa type, roughly every year and a half. Sometimes without much warning. Visa types have been eliminated (Compétences et Talents) and reconfigured (Passeport Talents).

I would therefore STRONGLY caution you against taking advice from random people on the internet who have experience only with their own visa, or who applied longer than 1 year ago. You should also consider whether the people offering advice submitted their application at the same consulate or VFS office as you will, or at the same préfecture. While the standards and general guidelines are the same, the *application* of those guidelines by thousands of people across hundreds of offices in France and around the world can be vastly different. Even factors like nationality, and quotas, and the time of year you apply can have an impact on your file and its processing time, outside of the overall quality of your application.

Taking advice from non-professionals who are not invested in the outcome of something as important as your visa application and who do not remain informed of updates to legislation and visa application and renewal procedures can potentially jeopardize the success of your application. Proceed with caution if you are getting free advice on Facebook rather than professional advice from someone who deals regularly with multiple préfectures, consulates, and visa types.

Who (what nationalities) is this book for?

The guidance in this book can be used for successful visa applications in almost all countries. With that in mind, it's important to know that there are several countries that have special bilateral agreements with France, which means that those countries may have 1) special visa requirements or 2) quotas on the number of visas granted. These special agreements primarily concern former French colonies, especially countries in North or West Africa. Before choosing a visa type, you should verify that your home country does not have special requirements or agreements that limit your visa options.

For people from countries without special bilateral agreements with France, the rules about visas and how to apply are pretty much always the same; however, the choice about whether to award a visa or not to an individual, and how many visas to award to nationals of each country, and when, is always a political choice. It is one that individual consulates or consular officials may not have a lot of control over. For this reason, applicants from countries like the United States, Australia, or Canada may have a very easy time getting a visa approved for France. The French Foreign Ministry opts to give more visas to nationals from those countries because many French citizens also want to go to those countries to live and work. Citizens from countries that have a more lopsided exchange with France may have a more difficult time getting visas, as lower numbers of visas are granted to people from some nations. Many highly qualified Indian citizens, for example, seek visas and residency permits to work in STEM fields, and a fraction of those who are qualified actually obtain their visas successfully.

This book will therefore be most useful to people from countries that do NOT have a special agreement with France. Nationals or permanent residents of the United States, Canada, Australia, New Zealand, and the United Kingdom will benefit particularly from the contents of this book and its explanations. Nationals from other countries in North America, Asia, or non-French-speaking African countries may also benefit from its guidance.

Note that because US persons are obligated to file US tax declarations even while living outside of the US, I have included relevant tax information for US citizens and green card holders who will be required to declare their worldwide income to the IRS. The US tax information can obviously be disregarded by readers who have no ties to the US.

DISCLAIMER

This is very important. Although this book is called "Foolproof French Visas," the process of applying for a French visa is not actually 100% foolproof. Some 3 million visa applications are submitted at French consulates around the world each year, and only a fraction of those are successful. I have an excellent track record in successfully getting visas for my clients, there are several factors to be taken into consideration, including nationality and country of the application, the applicant's overall quality, and the mood of that particular consular official on that day. The consulate can reject your application for any reason, or for no reason at all. The only rejections they have to justify are those that involve the spouses of French citizens.

The book's title should NOT be considered a guarantee that you will get your visa, even if you follow all of the instructions in this book. Allison Lounes and Paris Unraveled are not legally liable for any costs or damages related to unsuccessful visa applications.

Schengen Travel Rules

France is part of the European Union (EU), the European Economic Area (EEA, or 'Espace Economique Européen en français) and the Schengen space. In this section, we will explore the travel rules for being in Schengen as a tourist, and when you will need a long-stay visa.

What is Schengen?

Schengen is a collection of 26 countries that have eliminated border controls between them in order to allow free movement and strengthen cross-border law enforcement. You will typically only present your passport and visa upon entry into the first Schengen country you travel to. If you leave Schengen to go to a non-Schengen country like Ireland or the UK, you will have to re-present your passport and visa to travel to those countries and again when you return to Schengen. Your days spent in Schengen are tracked and your passport is scanned and stamped at each point of entry to and exit from Schengen.

Countries in the Schengen space include Austria, Belgium, Czech Republic, Denmark, Estonia, Finland, France, Germany, Greece, Hungary, Iceland, Italy, Latvia, Liechtenstein, Lithuania, Luxembourg, Malta, Netherlands, Norway, Poland, Portugal, Slovakia, Slovenia, Spain, Sweden, and Switzerland.

When traveling between these countries, you should always have your passport and titre de séjour, but your documents will not necessarily be checked at the borders. Random checks are always possible, however, especially in the event of a security incident, so you should always have your papers. It is important to know that having a visa for one of these countries does not give you the ability to stay in the others without restriction.

Tourists who do not require a visa to travel within Schengen (Americans, Canadians, other nationalities who can travel on just a passport) can spend up to 90 days total out of 180 days in any or all Schengen countries without applying for a visa. This period is rolling. Handy online calculators can use your travel dates to ensure you don't overstay your welcome, and you can find them by googling 'Schengen trip calculator.'

Any day during which you spend partially in a Schengen country counts as a day spent in Schengen. For example, if you leave Paris on Monday to go to London, and return on Friday, your trip was 5 days, but you only spent 3 days (Tuesday, Wednesday, Thursday) completely outside of the Schengen area. In practice, overstaying by a couple of days isn't going to cause too many problems, especially for tourists traveling from visa-waiver countries. While theoretically passport control can look through your stamps, add up your days and fine you (or even ban you!), they aren't likely to do that without a good reason or a pattern of abusing the Schengen system.

Applying for a Long-Stay Visa after Schengen Travel

Applying for a visa of any kind (short stay or long stay) removes the limitations of the Schengen visa-free travel rules. For example, if you are enrolled in an academic program that starts in September, but want to spend the summer in France or in Europe, you can spend May 20-August 15 in Europe, apply for a long-stay visa in your home consulate on August 17, and return to France as soon as you receive your passport back in the mail. There is no waiting period between returning to your home country after tourism and applying for a visa and returning.

The only caveat is that if you have a pattern of overstaying your Schengen tourism travel dates, you can jeopardize your chances for a long-stay visa.

Arriving Early in Schengen

If you have a long-stay visa, you can arrive in France (or in Europe) before it officially starts, provided that you are able to travel to Europe visa-free. In that case, you will be considered a tourist upon arrival, and your visa rights (to work, for example) will start on the start date of your visa.

If you have a French visa, but arrive through another EU country, your border control stamp for proof of entry into Schengen will be from that EU country. Normally, there is no border control between the EU states, and so you will not have direct proof of entry into France. In that case, OFII assumes that you arrived in France within 5 days of your arrival into Schengen, unless you provide proof of the exact date of arrival (a train or plane ticket, for example).

Overstaying a Long-Stay Visa

If you do not plan on renewing your visa upon its expiration (or are not able to renew it), your visa automatically converts to tourist status upon expiration. Again, this is assuming that you are allowed to travel in Schengen on just your passport, without an official tourist visa. You are therefore allowed to stay up to 90 days beyond the end date of your visa in Schengen countries, but your status will be that of a tourist. You will not be allowed to work or receive any benefits, including unemployment or housing assistance, after the expiry date of your visa or titre de séjour.

Traveling in Schengen as a French Resident

While you are a French resident with a valid visa or titre de séjour, you can travel in other Schengen countries, but you remain limited to 90 days out of 180 days in every Schengen country except for France. In practice, there are no border controls between the EU states, and you may therefore "get away with" overstaying the 90 days in other countries. However, in order to maintain your visa status in France and ensure you are able to renew, you should keep a permanent residence and proof of address in France for the duration of your visa. Moving around too much even within France or spending too much time outside of France during the year can invalidate the terms of your visa.

Working in Schengen as a French Resident

Any work rights conferred by your long-stay visa are limited to France, especially before you obtain a 10-year resident card. If you are working for a French company, they may send you on work trips to other EU countries, and if you are a French autoentrepreneur, company, or profession libérale, you may bill clients in other EU countries. However, all of your taxes are still paid in France.

While having a 10-year resident card, a "carte bleue européenne," or a vie privée et familiale card may facilitate the process for working in another EU country, you would still need to apply for a work permit from the country where you want to work. Students who would like to do internships in another EU country would have to apply for the appropriate visa for that country, but can do so from the consulate in France. For example, an American student in Paris who wants to do an internship in Amsterdam would have to research the procedures for getting an intern visa, and apply either in the Dutch consulate in Paris, or directly on-site in Amsterdam (if the Netherlands allows for in-country visa applications).

Finally, be aware that getting a visa to live and/or work in another country may invalidate your French visa and therefore interrupt your continuous stay in France. If you are planning on applying for residency or naturalization, you should research how getting a visa for another Schengen country would impact your ability to maintain your French visa. French permanent residents with a 10 year carte de séjour can live and work outside of France for up to 3 years without giving up their rights to French residency. If you plan to move between EU countries, you may want to explore opportunities for residency or naturalization in one before moving to another.

Working in France with Another Schengen Country's Visa
Last year, I had a consultation with a potential client who had gotten rejected for a French visa, and had instead gone to Germany, where he applied for a freelancer visa on-site, before relocating to France, where he wanted to apply for a visa on-site. He was quite indignant when I told him that working in France on his German visa was not allowed.

If you live and work in another EU country on a visa, you are limited to 90 days out of 180 in France as a tourist. You may come to France on business trips through your company, or bill clients in France for services if you are a registered freelancer or business in another EU country, but you cannot use another country's visa to come live and work in France. In that case, you would have to apply for a French visa at the French consulate in the country where you live, and meet the conditions of the appropriate visa type.

Working Remotely
You may believe that you can circumvent France's rules on work visas by getting a visitor visa, maintaining your job in their home country, and having your salary paid directly

into a foreign bank account. You may even claim that since the job and the company are located outside of France, that technically they are not "working in France," which their visa status prohibits. Your local French consulate may even support this idea, as there is no visa type specifically for this kind of setup.

However, this is a very, very bad idea that will become very expensive for you to fix (if it's even possible) once various authorities catch on to what you are doing.

Working + being in France = working in France.

Being a "digital nomad" is not possible if you are in France for more than 90 days.

If you have a visa to live in France, you become a French tax resident. (The visa presupposes you will be in France for more than 183 days, as you cannot renew the visa without actually living in France for most of the time.) If you are a French tax resident, you are bound to pay French social charges and income taxes on your earned income (salary, business income) in France FIRST, before paying taxes to any other country. This means that regardless of who is paying you and for what work, you need to be set up to pay French social charges and income taxes on that income. Of course, getting set up too pay social charges and taxes requires a work visa and a contract, whether that's a work contract (salairé en mission) or a freelancer contract (autoentrepreneur).

Initially, you may get away with it, as it would indeed be difficult for France to know what deposits are being made to your foreign bank account. However, as a French resident, you are also bound to declare your worldwide income on your French taxes, even if you are not subjecting the income to tax in France. Eventually, the prefecture will ask to see your French tax returns and your bank statements. They may also request your US tax returns and bank statements. If you want to transfer large amounts of money, the bank will also want to know where the money is coming from and will ask you to prove that the income has been properly subjected to tax.

Furthermore, if the préfecture or your local tax office gets suspicious that you have income outside of France that is not being taxed properly, they will collaborate and request many documents from you and send you large, scary bills and penalties that you are going to be hard-pressed to prove you don't have to pay. Of all of the French administrations, URSSAF - the Union de Recouvrement des cotisation de Sécurité Sociale et des Allocations Familiales - is the scariest one to cross.

I cannot stress enough that if you plan on staying in France for more than a year or two, you should make every effort to ensure that you are working and/or running your business *legally* with regards to French laws and tax laws, to avoid all potential problems. However, if you are staying less than two years, or if you get a "long séjour temporaire" visa, working remotely may not catch up with you before you return to your home country. While I would NEVER advise you to do anything illegal, I would advise you to weigh the costs and efforts required to get a proper work visa, set up and close a business activity, and tax amounts you would pay against the benefits of doing everything by-the-book.

If there is even a *slight* chance you could stay in France longer than 2 years, I would advise you to do everything the right way from the beginning rather than get the visitor visa and try to fix it later. You can always leave and abandon the "right" visa if things don't work out, but it will be a long and painful process to try to "fix" your visa situation and make it right if you decide you want to stay long-term - or if you get caught doing things the "wrong" way. I often discuss these options with my clients in our *Franceformation* consultations.

Helpful Vocabulary

The French visa process is complex, and requires a bit of specialized vocabulary to understand all of the concepts you need to know. In this section, I've presented the most useful vocabulary for the visa, carte de séjour, and renewal process, to help you understand each visa type and the administrative processes you'll have to go through.

Visa, Carte de Séjour, Titre de Séjour

Tourist Visa

A "tourist visa" is a travel visa for a short-term stay, (Type "C" visa) and is usually required for people whose passports do not allow them to travel freely to France or Europe. Applicants must provide proof of resources and proof of work and strong ties to their home countries, to adequately demonstrate that they will return to their home countries and will not seek work in France. A "Long Stay Visitor" visa is NOT a tourist visa.

Americans, Canadians, and nationals from several other countries can travel to France without applying for a tourist visa. Starting in 2021, nationals who can travel visa-free (i.e. on just their passports) will have to file for a travel authorization in advance. This procedure, called ETIAS – European Travel Information and Authorization System – is not a visa per se, but is an electronic authorization filed online. It will cost about €7 and will be valid for 5 years for travel to all Schengen countries.

Travelers who are on passports, or who have a tourist visa, cannot apply for a long-stay visa in France. The ONLY exception is for spouses of French or EU nationals who do not apply for visas before arriving in France, and who can regularize their situation by paying a fee. Even in that situation, it is usually preferable to return to your home country for a long-stay visa, as the prefecture is not always aware of how to process these arrivals, and the timeline for receiving a carte de séjour and its accompanying work permit can extend to several months.

Long-Stay Visa, or Visa Long Séjour

A visa is a travel document issued by a consulate that allows you to spend a certain amount of time in a country. There are many several different types of visas, but for the most part, we will be addressing the "Long Stay" or "Type D" visas, which are for people wanting to spend a year or more in France. A "Long séjour temporaire" is the only visa type that cannot be renewed or extended at all, under any circumstances, in France.

Because there are so many different types of "Long Stay" visa, saying "Long Stay" is not helpful to understanding what rights and obligations you have as a visa holder. Any visa you receive from the French consulate should indicate what type of visa it is, and what type of work it authorizes you to do. We will cover each type of Long Stay visa in this book.

VLS-VTS

This is short for a "Visa Long Séjour Valant Titre de Séjour." If you have a renewable long-stay visa (all D types except "Long Séjour Temporaire," you have a VLS-VTS. This means that you will complete the OFII procedures (discussed in Part III) upon arrival, potentially completing a medical visit and integration visit (depending on your visa type) and receiving an OFII validation form which will be required to renew your visa. After you have completed the OFII procedures, your visa is officially your "titre de séjour," or initial residency permit.

OFII Validation

OFII is the Office Français d'Immigration et d'Intégration, and the majority of foreigners arriving in France for immigration purposes are required to register with OFII within the first 90 days to validate their visas. When you arrive in France, you will need to register your arrival and provide an address to OFII as soon as possible. In practice, it sometimes takes a bit longer to get an appointment. You will be summoned for a medical visit, and depending on your visa type, you may also be summoned to an "integration day," where you learn about living in France and your rights and responsibilities as a French resident.

Since 2019, the OFII procedure is begun online, and the OFII tax is paid with a timbre fiscal purchased during the initial registration process. You do not have to bring purchased stamps to your appointment.

After completing the necessary appointments, you will provide certain documents (proof of address, proof of completing the OFII visits) to validate your OFII procedure and create your official 'titre de séjour' or legal proof of residency. This procedure is necessary for renewing your visa.

Some visa holders, like students, some passeport talent holders, and spouses of EU citizens, are no longer required to complete OFII procedures in-person and can validate their visas simply by purchasing the timbre fiscal and submitting a form online.

PRO TIP: Save a scan or a copy of your visa, passport control stamp showing your date of arrival in France, OFII document, and passport ID page in case any of these documents are lost or stolen.

Titre de Séjour or Carte de Séjour ?

A titre de séjour is your legal proof of residency, and this can take the form of either your original visa, or a plastic card to carry in your wallet, issued after your first renewal, called a "carte de séjour."

The OFII validation process transforms your visa into a titre de séjour, which can be renewed. Renewing your titre de séjour at the prefecture causes them to issue you the plastic carte de séjour.

In this book, I will use the term "visa renewal" or "change of visa status" to refer to the process by which you extend your initial visa or get a new valid carte de séjour from the prefecture. The terms visa, carte de séjour, and titre de séjour can be used interchangeably throughout, as they all relate to the document proving your legal ability to reside in France.

Récipissé

A récipissé is a paper receipt with your personal information and picture, which you receive when your titre de séjour is expiring. It extends the validity of your titre de séjour for a period of 3-4 months while you await your renewal appointment or while your carte de séjour is being produced. It also enables you to continue working or to receive benefits from the government that require a valid titre de séjour (unemployment or CAF benefits). If it is a récipissé for a renewal (but NOT for a "première demande), it also allows you to travel outside of France and return to the EU.

A récipissé should be given to you automatically at the end of your renewal appointment, to carry you through to when your new carte de séjour arrives.

If you make an appointment for a visa renewal, and the appointment falls *after* your titre de séjour expires, don't worry. It happens all the time. It is NOT required to get a récipissé if your titre de séjour is expiring or expired, provided that you have a convocation for a renewal appointment. If you are staying in France and do not plan on traveling between your card's expiration date and your renewal appointment, you can use the convocation along with your expired card to demonstrate your ability to stay in France.

However, if you prefer to have a récipissé to make things official, or if you need one for your employer, to travel outside of the EU, or certain benefits, you can bring your expiring titre de séjour, your convocation for your renewal appointment, a set of ID photos, and proof of address to the Centre de Réception des Etrangers at your local prefecture or sous-prefecture to have them make you one a week or two before your card expires. The process should be quick and easy.

Once you have renewed your titre de séjour and are awaiting your plastic card, you should receive notice to pick it up within the 3-month récipissé period. However, if the récipissé's expiration date is approaching and you would like another one, you can also return to the Centre de Réception des Etrangers with your expired card, récipissé, and ID photos, and have them make another one for you. Occasionally, and in certain departments, card production can take longer than the 3 months, especially at certain busy times of the year.

A récipissé must always be carried with your expired carte de séjour or titre de séjour to be valid. You should also always make a copy or a scan of your titre de séjour (both sides) and your current récipissé in case either is lost or stolen.

Convocation

A convocation is an official invitation or summons for you to present yourself for an administrative appointment. It includes your name, visa number, and the date, time, and place of the appointment. You will receive several of these throughout your time in France. A convocation should be considered like a subpoena. You do not want to miss the appointments on it.

(You won't be arrested if you don't comply, but it won't be pleasant to try to sort out the mess of making new appointments you missed.)

OFII Convocations: Once you submit your information to OFII for the OFII validation procedure, you will receive a series of convocations for the medical visit, integration day (if required), and the final validation of your visa where the affix the vignette in your passport.

Normally, you cannot choose the date and time of your convocation. If you MUST miss an appointment, because you're traveling, for example, you should go *in person* to your OFII office as soon as possible to make a new appointment. They will reschedule you one time. If you miss the second convocation for any reason, they will normally refuse to schedule you a third time, meaning that you must return to your home country and apply for a new visa. You are not able to validate, extend, or renew your visa without completing the OFII validation procedure.

Visa Renewal Convocations: When you make an appointment to renew your titre de séjour, you will receive a convocation (which you download when you make the appointment online, or which is emailed to you) with the date, time, and place of the appointment. When you arrive at your appointment, you will need to present the convocation along with your passport, titre de séjour, and other documents to receive a ticket to go to the guichet (window) and present your documents.

If your appointment is after your card expires, you can use the convocation as proof you are still in France legally, or use it to get a récipissé to extend the validity of your expired titre de séjour. It is very normal to have your visa appointment and convocation be *after* the expiry date of your visa, so don't worry if you're not able to secure an appointment within the recommended timeframe. It is the date you make the appointment and the fact that you make it before your titre de séjour's expiration date that matters.

Première Demande versus Renouvellement

When you renew your visa status and keep the same status, the process is called a "renouvellement." It is administratively very simple, and you typically have to provide exactly the same documents that you provided during your initial visa request. You can refer to the checklists in each visa section, and you will also be provided with a list by the prefecture when they issue the convocation. Window agents are generally very good about highlighting and explaining the documents you will need to provide, and at annotating with anything you need to add for your particular case. A récipissé for a renewal allows you to travel outside of the EU and to continue enjoying the same rights as your current visa type while you are waiting for your old card.

A "première demande" is the procedure for changing your visa type from one status to another, and is more administratively complex and time-consuming. The assumption under a première demande is that you maintain your former visa status until you are approved for the new type. Approval can happen on the spot during your appointment for some visa types, while other visa types require you to wait for notification from the prefecture that your request has been approved.

For example, a student who has been in France for several years and who marries a French person would request a "première demande" of a "vie privée et familiae" visa at her first appointment after the marriage. She would have to indicate that it was a change of status while making the appointment, which sometimes requires an in-person appearance or making a phone call rather than using the automated appointment system some prefectures have instituted online. At the appointment, she would submit documents showing proof of her eligibility for the new visa type (marriage certificate, livret de famille, proof of common residence with her spouse, etc.). She would be issued a récipissé that continues her student status at the end of her appointment, and therefore would not receive full rights to work, start a business, etc. until her new carte de séjour has been approved.

Alternatively, a master's graduate on a Recherche d'emploi visa who would like to switch to a "profession libérale" visa in order to freelance may receive tentative approval for a change of visa status at the initial "première demande" appointment. In this case, the window agent may approve a récipissé indicating the new status in order to enable the visa holder to formally register the business and to start having clients. She would then be invited back 2-3 months later with proof of the business registration and any contracts that have been established in order to get final approval of the new visa status.

French Consulates & VFS Global

A consulate is a branch of the French embassy that issues visas based on whether or not you meet the criteria for a certain visa type. Since 2018, French consulates in the US and Canada, as well as several other countries, have outsourced processing of visas to a company called VFS Global. VFS is a third-party company which accepts visa applications on behalf of the French embassy and consulates and forwards them on for processing.

VFS is not a French government entity, and as such, the transition from visa processing by the consulates to visa processing by VFS has been rocky and not without issues. In many cases, VFS agents cannot answer questions about visa requests or applications and cannot indicate which documents are necessary. Because they merely pass along documents for processing elsewhere, they are not reliable sources of information for what you need to provide. When dealing with VFS, it is advisable to submit ALL documentation you have and that is indicated in the checklists in this book. It is better for you to submit additional, unnecessary documents, rather than to have your application refused because the agent didn't ask for certain documents. YOU are responsible for knowing what is required and for making sure the application they accept is complete and thorough.

Furthermore, VFS and the France Visas website do not provide a complete list of documents until AFTER you have created and finalized a visa application online. But, you cannot complete the visa application form on their website without indicating which visa you are applying for. And, how can you know you are applying for the correct visa type and have all of the appropriate documents without being able to see the list? In my experience, the "numérisation" (digitalization) of this process has worsened the quality of the service provided by the consulates and VFS and causes ongoing confusion to visa applicants.

On more than one occasion, I have received an inaccurate supporting document list from the France-Visas website and had to write attestations or explanations for clients who were "missing" documents not on the list because the documents didn't apply to their situation. When VFS threatened to mark the file as incomplete, we provided a written note about why the list was incorrect and why they weren't included, but the situation certainly adds stress to any visa application.

Similarly, French consulates around the world often provide inadequate and contradictory information about which documents are required for each visa and its conditions for attribution. In my 6 years helping people get visas, I have dealt with all of the French consulates in the US and Canada, and those in several other countries around the world. With each visa application, I review the website of the specific consulate where my applicant will be applying. I am often appalled by the lack of information, or the fact that certain documents are requested in Houston, which are not required in Boston or San Francisco. Occasionally, information will appear on the website for the French consulate in Seoul or Mumbai which is not readily available to applicants in Montreal.

Moral of the story? Over-prepare, know what you need to provide for the type of visa you want, and make sure they take it all.

Préfectures & Sous-Préfectures

Upon arrival in France, the OFII validation process will be done through your regional OFII office, but your renewal will be processed in the regional prefecture, which is a division of the police department. Depending on the size of your department and the number of foreigners living there, the prefecture may have certain procedures (renewal appointment requests, document lists) available online. It may also outsource certain renewals (récipissés, 10 year cards, naturalization requests especially) to a local "sous-préfecture" rather than processing them in the main building.

It is important to know that different departments follow the same rules generally, but can have completely different procedures for making an appointment or submitting an application. In Paris, profession libérale applicants make an appointment first and submit their business plans and other supporting documents at the appointment. Conversely, in Bordeaux, applicants must submit completed business plans and project descriptions by mail before receiving an appointment for a change of status. Knowing or being able to research the rules and procedures for your specific department is essential to minimizing the stress of the bureaucratic process.

Comparing & Evaluating Long-Stay Visa Types

The purpose of this book is to provide an overview of each type of visa for living in France, and to guide you on the conditions of eligibility for that visa type, how to get it, and what you can do with it. We will study each visa in-depth to showcase its advantages and disadvantages, and the different ways in which it can lead (or not) to long-term residency and naturalization.

The explanation for each visa type will provide clarification on each of the following topics, so you can easily compare the different requirements and the pros and cons of each type:

Health Insurance

Since 2016, every person residing regularly in France for more than 3 months has had the right to have their own health insurance in the French system through a program called PUMA, Protection Universelle MAladie. In this system, individuals are covered through their jobs or self-employment, and anyone who is not otherwise affiliated with French sécurité sociale can submit PUMA applications to their local CPAM, Caisse Primaire d'Assurance Maladie. The process for applying for PUMA through the individual caisse will be explained for each visa type, as the procedure can vary slightly.

The visa types in this book require a travel insurance policy for catastrophic coverage and repatriation.

Income & Savings Requirement

Most visas have a minimum requirement for financial resources, which can vary based on the visa type and the number of individuals in the family. The baseline for a long-stay visitor visa, without the ability to work, is about €1.200 per month for 12 months, the length for which the visa is issued. This amount (€14.400) corresponds to the net amount after social taxes for someone making minimum wage at a full-time job in France.

Work

Until you receive a resident card (10 year carte de séjour), a Vie Privée et Familiale (VPF) card, or are naturalized as a French citizen, the type of work you are allowed to do on each visa – and whether you are allowed to work *at all* is highly regulated. Salaried employees may not work as freelancers, and freelancers/self-employed people may not work as employees on standard work contracts. Salaried employees on salaried worker visas who want to change jobs must remain in their initial jobs for a certain length of time, or have their new employer sponsor them.

It is important not to rely on anecdotal and non-professional advice when choosing your visa type, and especially important not to assume that something not explicitly prohibited is allowed.

Do NOT assume that because one agency, or even one agent, tells you something is acceptable, that it is legal or even advisable. Work rights for foreigners fall under the jurisdiction of several agencies, none of which is equipped to completely advise you on your rights. Visas are awarded by the consulates outside of France, and validated by OFII, an agency which integrates foreigners arriving in France to work and which ensures that taxes have been paid on all foreign hires. Approval of work contracts, however, is overseen by **DIRECCTE**, the DIrection Régionale des Entreprises, de la Concurance, de la Consommation, du Travail, et de l'Emploi, which evaluates the content of each contract and whether the hiring company has done their due diligence in trying to hire someone who *already* has the right to work in France before sponsoring a foreigner. That's already 3 different bureaucratic government agencies with different rules, and none of their employees are trained in how the other agencies apply their own rules to foreign workers.

DIRECCTE also evaluates the viability of business plans of companies that want to open in France, and keeps track of workers on other visa types (student and au pair, for example) who have a work authorization based on their visa type, but who are restricted from full-time or self-employment.

Once you are a French tax resident (because you have a visa and spend more than 183 days in France in a calendar year), the local tax office will subject you to French taxation and determine how to apply the tax treaty between your home country and France to all of your income. All of these agencies will ultimately communicate with **URSSAF**, the Union de Recouvrement des cotisations de Sécurité Sociale et d'Allocations Familiales, and **CPAM**, the Caisse Primaire d'Assurance Maladie, to ensure you are paying social taxes appropriately in order to get universal health insurance coverage. (The "Universal" part means paying in is *not* optional.)

When you renew your visa, no matter what visa type you have, the prefecture is going to want to see your last 12 months of bank statements from France and your home country, as well as your French tax declaration. They, or the local tax office, can also ask for your tax declaration you made in your home country to ensure that all of your revenue has been properly reported and taxed, and so they can calculate that mandatory health insurance premium.

The agents de guichet (window agents) at the prefecture and their superiors who process visa renewals are trained to notice discrepancies between your visa type and the types of income and deposits showing up in your bank account. They are trained to ask questions about where your money comes from and where you are paying taxes on it. And they are trained to apply the rules strictly, without regard for individual circumstance or, "but someone on the internet told me that his prefecture in (other city) told him to do it this way."

You do not want to get into a situation where you are fighting with the prefecture to renew your visa, or fighting with the tax office about how you declared income from work you weren't really supposed to be doing due to your visa type. You're better off paying protection money to the Organizatsiya than trying to untangle a mess of fines and overdue social charges after you get hit by URSSAF. Believe me when I say it is cheaper and easier to do it right the first time, than to hire a lawyer to fix it down the line. It may take them a couple of years to process the information they share and to catch you, but if and when they do, you are going to regret all of your life choices.

All that to say, please heed what I tell you about the types of work you are allowed to do on each visa.

Taxation

Anyone who has a valid visa for France and who lives in France for more than 183 days out of 365 becomes a tax resident of France. Tax residency is based on a number of factors, including where you spend most of your time, where your family lives, where you return, and where the center of your personal and economic interests lies.

You should not assume that because you spend less than 183 days in France, that you are not a French tax resident.

French tax residents are required to report their worldwide income as taxable in France. This includes declaring any bank accounts, businesses, and trusts held outside of France, and any income to these accounts. The tax treaty between France and the country where these assets or this income is located determines where the income is taxed, how it is taxed, and what foreign income tax credits it is subject to.

As a general rule, while you are a French tax resident, your earned income – the income you earn through work, like salary or self-employment – will be subject to social charges and income tax in France first, and you will get credit in your home country (if you have to declare at all). Your passive income, from rentals, interest, dividends, capital gains, or pensions, will be taxed in the country where it is earned. Again, you should look to the specific agreements between France and your home country because each tax treaty is slightly different.

Maintaining & Renewing the Visa

Assuming a particular visa type is renewable (all visa types except for "long séjour temporaire" can be renewed at least once, for part or all of a year), you are expected to continue to meet the visa conditions and to provide sufficient proof and documentation in order to renew. This comes in several stages.

First, your visa is validated by the OFII (Office Français d'Immigration et d'Intégration) in your region. OFII will validate your work contract, or request proof of enrollment in your educational facility, or otherwise double-check whatever motive you have for obtaining your visa.

When you go to renew your visa, the prefecture will provide you with a list of necessary documents, which tend to be the same documents you used to apply for your visa type in the first place. They will require proof that you have executed the terms of your visa for the previous year, and that you will continue to do so for the upcoming year. If you are a student, for example, they will want grade reports, attendance reports, and proof of enrollment for the upcoming year. If you are a salaried employee, they'll want payslips for the past year, as well as an up-to-date copy of your work contract proving that you are still working in the same place.

If your situation changes during the year – you switch schools, or get let go from a job, or you get married or divorced – you'll have to provide proof of the new situation. Depending on how it affects your visa, you'll also have to anticipate the change and potentially apply for a change of status. It's important to always inquire how such a change would affect your visa *before* you approach your visa renewal appointment, to avoid surprises and complications with processing your file.

Paths to French Residency & Naturalization

While most work and family visa types can be renewed indefinitely until obtaining residency or being eligible for naturalization, some visas are not intended to establish residency. "Residency" is not just the fact of residing legally in France or even of being a tax resident. In this case, it is also the sense of having the right to remain in France indefinitely, regardless of your work situation. French residency means having a 10-year carte de résident, which is distinct from "tax residency" which is far easier to establish.

Some visa options (student, au pair, travailleur temporaire) are considered temporary, which means they can only be renewed a limited number of times, and you can only convert them to certain other visa types. These visas are designed for people who want to spend a short time in France or those who want to study or participate in a youth work exchange. Study and work exchange visas were created to enable young people to spend time living and working in another country, but they do not allow the holder to get a permanent job contract (CDI – contrat à durée indéterminée), establish a career, or meet the requirements for financial stability required for residency and naturalization.

For each visa type, I have indicated whether there is a limit to how many times it can be renewed, and in what circumstances, and when holders of that particular status can expect to receive a 10-year resident card or submit a successful naturalization application. For the visa types that cannot be renewed, or that can be extended only briefly, I have also indicated what changes of status are possible. If you would like to remain in France indefinitely, you should aim to avoid visa types that do not enable you to apply for residency or naturalization.

British Citizens Remaining in France After Brexit

At the time of this update in July 2020, it is still unclear what will happen when the UK leaves the European Union and British citizens in France no longer have the right to remain indefinitely on their UK passports. British expats in France hoped that the UK and the EU would reach a deal beneficial to both sides, but no deal was been reached. Without a deal, British citizens who want to live in France will have to abide by the same rules and regulations that apply to other third country nationals, with a grace period to allow British citizens in France to apply for residency permits before the new rules go into effect.

British citizens who wish to retain the right to remain in France must establish their residency in France before December 31, 2020, and will be required to have a French titre de séjour by July 1, 2021. Requests for residency permits can be submitted online beginning October 1, 2020.

Without a deal, a few things will happen.

1) British citizens who have been in France for more than 5 years can apply for a long-term residency card and/or apply for naturalization. Many Brits living in France are already doing this and getting their cartes de séjour which ensure they can stay in France. In order to receive a carte de résident, they will have to show they have been earning at least minimum wage (SMIC, €1.500 per month) or more,

However, certain people lived in France without properly setting up their businesses or declaring their income, and many claimed that they were still British tax residents, never admitting to living in France. Now, in many cases, their French taxable income is not high enough and they do not have enough documents justifying that they have been living as residents of France for 5 years. In some cases, people who have been living in France for many years will have to return to the UK.

2) British citizens who have been living in France for LESS than 5 years will have to apply for one of the visa types listed in this book. Those who already reside in France will not have to return to the UK to apply for a visa, but will instead be able to request a "carte de séjour" directly by submitting an application for a "première demande," with all of the documents in French.

As of the publication of the second edition of this book, the French government is working on releasing a website to enable British citizens to apply for their cartes de séjour directly through a specialized online portal. The site's release date has been pushed back from July 2020 due to complications from COVID, and its release is scheduled for October 1, 2020.

There are a few major consequences to this requirement. First, if a British person does not meet the requirements for that visa type, they will not be able to get a carte de séjour. For example, a woman who works only part-time and makes around €1.200 per month would not be able to get a salaried worker visa to continue in her current job. Even if she lives with a partner (if she lives with a French partner but is not married), and shares her expenses, her salary and her job description would not be sufficient for her company to sponsor her. Furthermore, the company that employs her would likely have to pay the OFII tax if they *are* able to sponsor her, which many employers would not do.

Similarly, British citizens will now be restricted to the type of employment authorized by the visa status they have. British students will be limited to 964 hours per year of work and would have to get a student, then APS, then salarié carte de séjour in order to earn the right to remain in France. While British citizens were previously able to have a salaried job, then quit to start their own business, and then take on a part-time CDD while still operating their business - now, they would have to change their visa status each time their employment situation changed, going from salarié, to profession libérale or commerçant, and then refuse the CDD or switch back to a salaried status - which is not easy! British citizens will no longer be able to pick and choose and cobble together different employment options as they were previously able to do.

3) British citizens who are not currently residing in France will have to apply for a long-stay visa prior to relocating. This final point is relatively straightforward, but prior to Brexit, British citizens could simply hop on the Eurostar with a suitcase on Sunday and begin working on Monday. This will no longer be the case after Brexit. British citizens hoping to relocate to France, as students or to work, will have to apply for one of the visa types contained in this book, and get a visa in their passport before moving. Upon arrival, they will be subject to the same OFII procedure as other non-EU nationals, and will have the same restrictions on their work authorizations.

In summary, British citizens applying for visas or cartes de séjour post-Brexit should be very careful to rely on information designed for non-EU nationals, and to disregard advice from EU citizens and Brits who relocated pre-Brexit. The rules and restrictions are going to be very different for recent arrivals than they were for those who arrived several years ago, and it will be very important to respect the conditions of the visa status or carte de séjour you receive if you would like to stay in France long-term and establish residency.

Spouses of British Citizens in France

Until December 31, 2020, spouses of British citizens who were not themselves EU citizens (e.g. an American married to a British citizen) are eligible to receive a Vie Privée et Familiale card for a duration of 5 years. Under the Brexit rules, spouses of British citizens established in France prior to December 31, 2020 will be able to apply for a titre de séjour under the existing rules.

Spouses arriving after the December 31 deadline will have to apply for their own visa type or be considered "visitors," similar to spouses of other third country nationals.

Brexit Procedures

All British citizens who have not yet submitted a request for a carte de séjour can doo so beginning on October 1, 2020 through this online portal: chttps://invite.contacts-demarches.interieur.gouv.fr/BREXIT/Mise-a-jour-du-site-de-demande-de-titre-en-ligne-pour-les-ressortissants-britanniques-residant-en-France

If you have already submitted a carte de séjour request through your local préfecture, you should be able to disregard this procedure.

The Facebook group RIFT - Remain In France Together is a great resource for British citizens remaining in France or relocating to France after Brexit. I am also able to consult and provide assistance in understanding your relocation options (see the Getting Help with Your Visa Application section at the end of the book.)

Remember that while you are living in France as a foreigner with a visa, you are not a citizen, and you do not have the same rights that you do in your home country to find work, start a business, quit your job, or do whatever the heck you want. Each visa type has its own rules and regulations, and whatever is not specifically authorized should be avoided without clarification.

For these retirement or temporary visa types, you should get a clear picture of what you are and are not allowed to do, what your opportunities for work, renewal, and naturalization will be, and whether or not that particular visa type will be a good fit for you. Keep in mind that no visa type will allow you to do EVERYTHING you want to do, unless you are entitled to a vie privée et familiale card or hold EU citizenship. But respecting your visa type's restrictions in the short-term will enable you to stay in France and gain permanent residency and the ability to do everything you want in the long term.

Non-Work Visas

This book is about the two main "non-work" visas. They are the long-stay visitor and the temporary long-stay visa, both of which are designed for people who intend to live in France without working. The main difference between them is that the regular "visitor" visa allows you to continue to renew your stay in France, and most importantly, makes you a French tax resident. Conversely, the "temporary long-stay" visa is just that - temporary, without the option to renew or extend the length of time you're allowed to stay in France.

These are both relatively simple visas to get, but you'll have to pay attention to how you assemble your application to ensure that you don't accidentally get a visa type you don't want. You don't want to end up with a "temporary stay" visa if you intend on staying in France for more than a year, and you don't want to end up with *either* of these types of visas if you actually want to work or do any income-producing activities. And neither of these visa types are ideal for getting on the path to French residency or naturalization.

Long Séjour Temporaire

The "long séjour temporaire" (LST) visa is, in my opinion, the least desirable visa type to get. It is also relatively new. The French consulates started issuing these visas unexpectedly to students planning to come to France for language classes, without publishing any information about this nonrenewable visa type that has very few advantages aside from the simple fact of allowing the bearer to remain in France for whatever length of time.

Since its inception, I have mostly advised people on how NOT to get stuck with a long séjour temporaire visa, as I think it's better to plan for a longer stay and keep the option of renewing the visa. You can always decide to go home if you choose not to renew your visa in France. But with the Long Séjour Temporaire visa, you CANNOT opt to renew or extend your stay under any circumstances.

The only advantage that comes to mind about the "long séjour temporaire" visa is the fact that it is exempt from OFII procedures, and it assumes you are going to be a tourist rather than a resident. Because you are not required to register with OFII and provide proof of address, you will likely be issued an LST visa if you indicate that you plan to move around a lot within France and stay in different regions. If you're staying on a boat that moves around, or planning to spend a few months in a couple of different cities, an LST visa will prevent you from going through the complex change-of-address or change-of-department process each time you move.

There don't appear to be any advantages in terms of tax residency or ability to work, but we'll explore that in the "Taxation" section of this chapter.

Visa Summary

Who is it for?
☑Anyone who wants to live in France temporarily, without working and who has the cash financial resources to be able to do so.

▫VFS Appointment Fee: $30
▫Application fee at Consulate: €99 (about $111 USD)
▫OFII fee: none - no OFII visit required.

▫Where to apply: In country of residence, at your local French consulate or VFS office.

▫Length of visa: up to 12 months

▫Renewal: None.

Path to residency and naturalization: None.

Health Insurance

As you will not be able to enroll in the French health system until you have been in France for more than 3 months, you will need a catastrophic coverage travel insurance policy in order to get your visa. The minimum coverage required for the visa is a travel policy with $50,000 of coverage with no deductible, as well as repatriation insurance.

In theory, it should be possible to enroll in the French healthcare system after living in France for 3 months on a valid visa. In practice, the limited and nonrenewable nature of the visa and the length of time required for obtaining coverage through the French system means that it's probably not worth it to begin the process for enrolling with CPAM unless you plan to return to France with a renewable visa type (if the LST is issued in error and you plan to request a new visa).

Income & Savings Requirement

This visa does not allow you to work, so any income you earn during your visa must be from passive sources, like investments or rental income, rather than from any type of work.

You will have to have savings of €1.200 per month for the entire length of your stay, or €14.400 in cash for a 12-month visa. If you do not have sufficient resources for a full year, your visa will be limited to the number of months for which you have resources.

Work

You are not allowed to do paid work with a long séjour

temporaire visa. This includes any type of remote work as an employee or contractor for companies outside of France. Because you cannot change your visa status, you cannot look for employment or plan to switch from an LST visa to any kind of work visa. You must be prepared to not do any income-producing activities while living in France on your LST visa.

Taxation

If you do not register with OFII, don't really establish a permanent place to live, and are not working per the terms of your visa, your information will likely not be transmitted to the local tax office or relevant tax services. Therefore, while you could be present in France for more than 183 days during a given tax year, triggering tax residency, leaving at the end of your visa and not returning means that the tax services will not be looking for a French tax declaration from you. It does NOT mean that you aren't *supposed* to complete a declaration if you meet the criteria for being a French tax resident. It simply means you may get away with not doing so if you leave and don't return to France. You could theoretically make the argument that the "temporary" status of this visa implies that you do not establish tax residency, but that would be a topic to discuss during a paid consultation with a certified accountant (expert-comptable) who can advise you appropriately.

Many people inadvertently get the LST visa while intending to prolong their stay in France and establish residency, and therefore return to their home countries at the end of their

LST visa to reapply for another, more appropriate visa type right away. In that case, you should begin filing French tax declarations for the first calendar year during which you were in France for more than 183 days. Therefore, if you arrive in France with an LST visa in April, 2019, and return to your home country in March, 2020 to reapply for a new visa type, and return to France with a different visa in June, 2020, you should file a French tax declaration for 2019 and 2020, with your worldwide income from all sources.

Maintaining and Renewing Your Visa

The Long Séjour Temporaire visa is not extendable or renewable in France. The end date on your visa is the date by which you must leave French territory.

Establishing Residency

Because you are required to leave by the end of your visa and must get a new visa in your home country to return to France, you will not be able to establish residency or count any time spent with a "Long Séjour Temporaire" status towards residency or naturalization. The clock on your continuous time spent in France will restart with each new LST visa, or with the new visa type you get after returning home after your LST status ends.

Family Members

An accompanying spouse or family members can get long-stay visitors visas and are subject to "regroupement familial" procedures.

Pros & Cons

☑ Enables you to live in France for a set period of time, up to 12 months, without working.

✗ You must prove you can support yourself financially with €1200 per month of cash resources.
✗ You CANNOT work for anyone, anywhere. You cannot work in France, you cannot work remotely for a company abroad, you cannot work for clients on the moon, regardless of where the bank account and the clients are.
✗ Does not provide a path to residency or naturalization.
✗ Impossible to switch status or extend the visa in France.

Documents to Provide for Application

☑ Convocation for a visa appointment at consulate or VFS center
☑ A cover letter explaining the purpose of your move
☑ Long-stay visa application, completed through France Visas
☑ Proof of financial resources
☑ Place to stay for first few weeks upon arrival
☑ Plane ticket & departure date
☑ Proof of 12 months of catastrophic health and repatriation insurance
☑ Financial resources of approximately €1.200 per month of your stay (about €15.000) in *cash*
☑ Name change and divorce/separation documents (if applicable)

Long-Stay Visitor Visa

Beware of the long-stay visitor visa if you are not retired. The long-stay visitor visa allows you to live in France without working for 12 months, and can be renewed yearly as long as you can continue to support yourself on your own cash resources. It does not allow you to work, but it does allow you to get into the French healthcare system through PUMA. In fact, you will be required to pay a PUMA cotisation based on your income, even if you keep your private insurance.

Why should you avoid this visa type if you are not retired? Simply because it is very difficult, if not impossible, to switch to another visa type. When allowed, changing your visa status from visitor to something else s a very long process that requires renewing your visitor status at least once for an additional year before you can make an appointment to switch. During the change of status process, the préfecture will scrutinize your reasons for applying for the visitor visa in the first place, and can revoke your status entirely if it finds that you were not abiding by the terms of your visa or that you came with fraudulent intentions that you did not declare to the consulate.

Do not apply for a visitor visa with the intention of looking for a job. Do not apply for a visitor visa with the intention of taking time to start a business or a company. Do not apply for a visitor visa with the intention of working remotely. And do not apply for a visitor visa under the delusion that you will be able to easily change statuses once you figure out what it is you really want to do. A visitor visa is not the first step in any plan to move to France long-term, unless you are retired. Carefully consider how a visitor visa would fit into your actual long-term plans before applying for one.

I worked with a client for nearly 2 years to switch her status from visitor to profession libérale so she could be a photographer, and that was after she had already made the attempt to switch with another immigration professional. During that time, she was not able to work legally, which impacted her mental health and her ability to support herself. Part of the reason for the long timeline was her application's initial rejection when the préfecture suspected she had been working when it wasn't authorized. Fortunately, she is now thriving.

The visitor visa is designed first and foremost for retirees who can support themselves on their cash resources and pension income and who do not intend to work, and who will likely never gain the ability to work or be naturalized French. If this is you, you will gain access to a great (and inexpensive) healthcare system in a country with a relatively low cost of living, without paying too much in taxes.

Visa Summary

Who is it for?
☑Anyone who wants to live in France without working and

who has the cash financial resources to be able to do so.

VFS Appointment Fee: $30
Application fee at Consulate: €99 (about $111 USD)
OFII fee: €225

Where to apply: In country of residence, at your local French consulate or VFS office.

Length of visa: 12 months

Renewal: in 1 year increments

Path to residency and naturalization:
After renewing for 5 years, you *MAY* receive a 10 year carte de résident, but it will very likely still have the mention "visiteur" and not enable you to work. This visa does not provide a clear path to full residency. Getting a 10 year card is subjective and depends on the area where you apply.
You can apply for naturalization by decree after 5 years, but if you have not been paying French taxes (e.g. you do not have earned income taxed in France), you are unlikely to be naturalized.

Health Insurance

As you will not be able to enroll in the French health system until you have been in France for more than 3 months, you will need a catastrophic coverage travel insurance policy in order to get your visa. The minimum coverage required for the visa is a long-stay visa policy for 12 months with $50,000 of coverage with no deductible, as well as repatriation insurance.

You can enroll in the French healthcare system after living in France for 3 months on a valid visa. If you are not working in France and therefore contributing to the French system through employee social tax contributions, you will be assessed an 8% tax called a PUMA cotisation (Protection Universelle MAladie) or health insurance premium. This will be on ALL income over €10.000 *except* for government pensions. This means that if you are retired and receive US social security, it would not be taxed, but income from IRAs, 401Ks, company pensions, rental income, other passive investments, etc. would be taxed. PUMA cotisations are individual, so if you are moving with your spouse, you will be assessed and pay separately based on your individual incomes. If your PUMA-eligible income is very low, you may not pay for PUMA at all.

Note that maintaining private health coverage will NOT exempt you from paying the PUMA insurance premium, so it makes sense to cancel your private coverage once you are in the French system. It may take the better part of a year before you are assessed the PUMA fee.

US Medicare: American retirees who are eligible for Medicare should carefully consider which "parts" they will sign up for before moving to France. Because you cannot use Medicare while living in France, this would mostly apply to any healthcare you expect to receive in the US, or whether you plan to move back to the US at some point later in life. Once you cancel certain "parts" of Medicare, if you plan to re-enroll for them, you will pay a penalty on your Medicare contribution each month that you are enrolled in that part, for the rest of your Medicare eligibility (the rest of your life.) Consider your likelihood of returning to the US and using Medicare and the cost of canceling Part B versus continuing to pay for it without using it in anticipation of your return.

Income & Savings Requirement

An adult on a long-stay visitor visa must have approximately €1.200 per month in cash resources, or about €15.000 total for the year. This amount must be in cash and cannot be in investments, CDs, or other inaccessible funds.

If you do not have sufficient resources for a full year, your visa will be limited to the number of months for which you have resources, and you will likely get a "long séjour temporaire" visa from the previous section.

You are only allowed to count income from passive sources (pension income, interest and dividends, rental income) towards your means of financial support if you are officially retired. Otherwise, you can only count your cash resources.

Because you are not allowed to work in France, you should not plan on counting any business income or salary towards your financial resources. In fact, agents at your renewal appointment will request to see your French and US bank statements, and will pay special attention to any odd deposits that make it look like you are working for compensation. Be aware that even if the consulate waves it off, your income on this visa type will still be scrutinized at a later date.

Work

You are not allowed to work on a visitor visa. This means that you are not allowed to do any active income-producing activities for anyone, anywhere in the world. You cannot work remotely. You cannot work for clients outside of France, whether they are in your home country, in China, or on the Moon.

If you are working in France, whether it's a salaried position or self-employment, and you do not have the appropriate visa status, you are violating the conditions of your visitor visa. If social taxes are not being paid on your income, you (and potentially your employer) are going to be in a world of trouble with URSSAF (French agency that collects taxes on earned income) when they find out.

Because you cannot easily change your visa status, you cannot look for employment or plan to switch from a visitor visa to any kind of work visa. You must be prepared to not do any income-producing activities while living in France on your visitor visa, and to maintain the visitor status for at least 2 years before you can consider switching to another visa type. Otherwise, you must return to your home country to apply for a new, different kind of visa.

Don't do it. You won't get away with it forever.

Taxation

Having a visa to live in France for more than 183 days makes you a French tax resident, which means you will need to declare your worldwide income on your French tax declaration. However, this does not mean that you will necessarily pay French taxes.

For expats and dual citizens who have financial interests in multiple countries, where you pay tax and what you pay it on is largely governed by the tax treaty between France and your home country (or the country where you have your other financial assets.) As a general rule, EARNED income (e.g. salary or income from a business where you actively work) is taxed in the country where you live and are a tax resident. This is why residing in France but "working" remotely in another country does NOT exempt you from paying French tax on that income.

Conversely, income-producing property is generally taxed in the country where it is located. If you have two rental properties, one in France and one in the US, the French property would be taxed first in France, and income from the US property would be taxed in the US.

Depending on your country's tax treaty with France, you may get a French tax credit for *taxes* paid on the income in the other country, or you may get a French tax credit for *the amount of French tax you would have paid had the income been subject to tax in France.*

Finally, it's important to know that all of your worldwide income will "count" towards determining your French tax rate on the income that *is* taxed in France. So, for example, if you have pensions, interest and dividends from the US (which are not taxed in France) and ALSO have salary or autoentrepreneur income in France, you'll be in a higher tax bracket and pay a higher tax rate because of your untaxed income increasing your marginal tax rate.

Also note that income taxes are separate from social charges and the PUMA (health insurance) premium, and will be assessed independently. Exemption from paying French income taxes on non-French income does not exempt you from other kinds of French tax.

Estate Planning

French laws about estates and successions are VERY specific, and you should take them into consideration before making France your residence. If you are retired or elderly, and there is a possibility that you could die as a French resident, you should be aware that your residency will determine the laws that apply to your estate. Estate taxes are relatively high, and would apply to your worldwide estate and financial assets, except real property like houses.

The two main things you will have to consider are your marital regime (community property or separate property) and your successors. Unless you specifically declare otherwise, your marital regime is determined by your first marital domicile - the state or country where you first lived with your spouse as a married couple. The laws of that jurisdiction will normally determine how you share property with your spouse and how it passes from one of you to the other (and whether there is gift tax between spouses). You should work with a French notaire experienced in international wills and estates to determine exactly what your situation is.

Similarly, unless you specify otherwise, French law will apply to your estate. French residents who are nationals of other countries can now elect to have their home country's law apply to their estates, but this requires a formal declaration and filing a will officially with a French notaire. Even then, you may not be able to do certain things, like disinherit one of your children (not allowed in France in most circumstances) and you should plan with a notaire accordingly to ensure your wishes are respected.

Finally, you should make plans regarding burial or cremation, and whether you would want to have your body repatriated.

Maintaining and Renewing Your Visa

As long as you continue to abide by the terms of your visa (without working) and have sufficient financial resources, you should be able to continually renew your titre de séjour in France without returning to your home country.

You may have problems renewing if it is discovered that you are working or illegally operating a business from France, or if you do not establish a fixed residence while you are here. Moving around too much can also disqualify you from renewal, because you are supposed to have a permanent address, which you will need for all administrative procedures and the OFII and préfecture visits.

Changing your status from a visitor visa to something else is going to be quite difficult. Do NOT come on a visitor visa with the expectation of changing to another status, because you will not be able to do so before you have been in France for at least two years.

If you arrive in France and decide you would like to have a different status, one option is to go home to your home country and apply for a new (different) kind of visa. Obviously you will have to meet the criteria for that new visa type, and you will lose any time you have accumulated in France towards residency.

Your other option is to ensure you have renewed your visitor visa at least once and received your new carte de séjour valid for one year. Once you receive the new card (you have picked it up from the préfecture and have it in your hand), you can make an appointment with the appropriate office and request a change of visa status, for example, from visitor to profession libérale.

The downside of this approach is that the process can take a VERY long time. If you arrive in France in June 2019 on a visitor visa, and have your renewal appointment in June 2020, you can expect to receive your renewed carte de séjour around September or October 2020. Once you have received the new card, you can THEN make an appointment, which will be another 2-3 months away, depending on availability. This means that you will be able to apply for your new status around January 2021, and receive approval for your new status around March or April 2021. It is much quicker to return home and apply for a different visa unless you have already renewed your current status at least one time.

Establishing Residency

You'll establish tax residency during the first year, but getting an actual residency permit after living in France for 5 years will be discretionary and subject to approval by the préfecture. Some people seem to believe that someone can come to France, hang out for 5 years as a visitor, and then get a long-term residency card that affords full work rights, but that is rarely the case. It is very likely that you will receive a "visitor" residency card (if you even get a longer carte de séjour) which will not allow you to work.

Better to come to France with a different status or change your status to get actual residency.

You will have a similar problem if you're considering naturalization. Although you will declare your worldwide income on your French tax return, you are unlikely to be paying much, if anything, in French income taxes if you do not have French salary or business income. Most retired expats in France pay zero income taxes. Because financial stability and your history of paying French taxes are taken into account during your naturalization application, it can be quite difficult to become French nationals if you have not paid income tax. (You will, of course, pay many other kinds of tax, like taxe d'habitation, VAT, and more.)

Family Members

An accompanying spouse or family members can get long-stay visitors visas and are subject to "regroupement familial" procedures.

Pros & Cons

Pros:
☑ Enables you to live in France and to continue renewing your visa as long as you can continue to support yourself without working.

Cons:
✗ You must prove you can support yourself financially with €1200 per month of cash resources.

✗You CANNOT work for anyone, anywhere. You cannot work in France, you cannot work remotely for a company abroad, you cannot work for clients on the moon, regardless of where the bank account and the clients are.

✗Does not provide a clear path to residency or naturalization.

✗Not easy to switch status in France; a switch is impossible before the first renewal.

Documents to Provide for Application

☑Convocation for a visa appointment at consulate or VFS center

☑A cover letter explaining the purpose of your move

☑Long-stay visa application, completed through France Visas

☑Proof of financial resources

☑Place to stay for first few weeks upon arrival

☑Plane ticket & departure date

☑Proof of 12 months of catastrophic health and repatriation insurance

☑Financial resources of approximately €1200 per month of your stay (about €15.000) in *cash*

☑Name change and divorce/separation documents (if applicable)

Documents to Provide for Renewal

☑Convocation for a renewal appointment at the local préfecture

- ☑ Attestation of OFII visit, and titre de séjour
- ☑ Set of ANTS standard passport photos, usually from a Photomaton machine
- ☑ CERFA form provided by the information desk when you arrive at your appointment
- ☑ Proof of residence less than 3 months old (justificatif de domicile)
- ☑ Proof of health coverage
- ☑ Birth certificate with certified translation
- ☑ Proof of financial resources of approximately €1200 per month of your stay (about €15.000) in *cash*, including all bank statements for French bank account and account in your home country
- ☑ Name change and divorce/separation documents (if applicable)
- ☑ Most recent French tax declaration, and tax bill (avis d'impôts sur le revenu) if available
- ☑ Signed statement saying you will not work or seek employment in France

Applying for a French Visa

Once you've figured out what type of visa you need and approximately when you would like to arrive in France, you can begin gathering the documents for your application.

The flaw in the new "and improved" system is that the French consulates no longer provide lists of documents and requirements for each visa type directly on their website. And while the France-Visas website provides a minimal list of what you'll need (don't trust it to tell the full story), they don't give you the list until AFTER you have completed and finalized your long-stay visa application form. This essentially means that you have to choose your visa type and the length of your stay BEFORE they'll give you the list and tell you whether or not you're even going to be able to get the visa in question.

For each visa type in this book, I've provided a suggested list of documents, which you should use along with the France-Visas "official" list to assemble your application. Be advise that both of these lists are guidelines and are the *minimum* that should be provided to have your visa approved; having a complete application per these lists does not guarantee approval. Be sure to compare the list I've provided in this book to the official list you receive from France-Visas or from the préfecture, and to have everything on both lists for your appointment. Better to go to your appointment over-prepared than to be turned away for not having a document you didn't know you needed!

Documents You May Need

YOUR PASSPORT

You will need a valid passport with available blank pages, and **you will need to submit your original passport to the VFS office for them to affix the visa**. This means you will be without your passport and unable to travel from the time you submit your visa application until the time it is returned to you, typically about 2-3 weeks maximum. If you need to travel while the French embassy is processing your visa application, it is usually possible to request an emergency second passport, valid for a period of 2 years.

Please ensure that your passport is valid for at least 6 months beyond the end date of the visa you are applying for. If you are applying for a 1-year visa, your passport should be valid for at least 18 months beyond your visa's proposed start date. Please also ensure that the name on your passport is the same as your name on your other documents.

If you are in France and applying for a renewal or change of visa status, you will have to bring your original passport to each appointment with you, but you will never have to leave your original passport at the préfecture. Instead, the préfecture will likely ask you to provide a photocopy of each page of your passport, including your ID page, your visa page, and each page that shows an entry or exit stamp into the Schengen space.

Basic Administrative Documents:

- ✓ 2 passport photos, standardized ANTS-format photos. The photo should be 35 mm wide and 45 mm high. The size of the face should be 32 to 36 mm (70 to 80% of the picture) from chin to forehead (excluding hair). You can have these pictures taken with the proper format at the VFS Global office for $12.
- ✓ Your valid carte de séjour, if you are in France
- ✓ Your Long-Stay Visa application, completed via france-visas.gouv.fr.
- ✓ Your visa appointment confirmation from VFS.
- ✓ If you are in France: your convocation for your appointment at the préfecture. Please verify that all information on the convocation is correct (name, AGDREF number).

Cover Letter:

For most visas, I find it very useful to provide a one-page cover letter outlining the reasons for the application and move to France, your means of financial support, and the activities you intend to undertake while in France. If you are applying for your visa outside of France, you can write this in the language of the country you are applying from, or in English.

Travel & Means of Support Documents:
Temporary emergency health insurance. You need

catastrophic health coverage for 12 months; It must be a policy appropriate for 365 days of travel, cover all of the EU/Schengen space, and have $50,000 of coverage with no deductible. Not applicable if you are a student under 28, on a salaried work visa, or the spouse of a French citizen.

Bank Account Statement. You need to show adequate means of financial support during your stay in France. Different types of visas have different financial requirements, depending on whether you are able to work. If you have both French and US accounts, provide recent statements for both.

Plane ticket with expected departure date. Visa processing times are 10-15 business days. If you're not sure exactly how long your visa will take to process, you can provide this document as a follow-up once your visa is ready to be issued. Your departure date should be no more than 90 days after your visa appointment date.

Proof of place to stay for first month or so upon arrival.
1. If you have a friend or family member who has a residence near where you'll be staying, you can put that person's address and indicate that you'll be staying there 'while looking for permanent housing.'
2. You can do a long-term lease through a trusted agency that works with expats, such as Vingt Paris. They will give you a proper lease, and none of my clients have ever had an issue with them. I am not

affiliated with them in any way.
3. You can rent an Airbnb, hotel room, or hostel room for the first 3-4 weeks, so you have a place to stay upon arrival while you look for a permanent apartment. Note that you will not be able to do many administrative formalities until you have a permanent place to live.

Criminal Background Check:
You no longer have to get a criminal background check before applying for French visas. VFS will take your fingerprints at the time of your appointment.

If you are applying for visas for minor children:
- ✓ A long stay visa application for each individual, including children
- ✓ Passport photos for the children
- ✓ Certified copies of their birth certificates
- ✓ Documents showing full custody, or notarized agreement from the children's other parent that you can move them to France

If you are married, or have previously been married:
- ✓ Your marriage certificate
- ✓ A livret de famille, if your spouse (current or former) is/was a French citizen
- ✓ Divorce papers or death certificate for former spouse
- ✓ Any papers or documents regarding name changes

If you are a Student:
- ✓ CampusFrance forms completed, submitted, and validated. (3 weeks for regular service, or 3 business days for "rush service" for an additional $150 fee.)
- ✓ Receipt for payment to CampusFrance.
- ✓ Certificate of pre-enrollment from school.
- ✓ Curriculum vitae or résumé
- ✓ Certificates and transcripts from all trainings and degree programs
- ✓ High school, college, and graduate diplomas
- ✓ Financial Guarantee: If you are on a STUDENT or VISITOR visa and you do not have sufficient financial resources on your own, you will need a notarized financial guarantee from a family member. You CANNOT work or make reference to any earned income when applying for these visa types.

If you are starting a business (artist, profession libérale, commerçant, or passeport talents - entrepreneur visas):
- ✓ Curriculum vitae or résumé
- ✓ Certificates and transcripts from all trainings and degree programs
- ✓ High school, college, and graduate diplomas
- ✓ Allison will provide you with all of these documents if you are a Franceformation client. The documents will be provided in English if you are applying for a visa processed by VFS in your home country, or in

French if you are applying for a change of status within France. To get guidance on writing the plan yourself, you can discuss enrolling in the Complete French Business Incubator.

- ✓ Cover letter
- ✓ Business plan
- ✓ 3 years of financial projections
- ✓ Letters of support and collaboration from past, present, and future clients, or professionals with whom you may partner.
- ✓ Proposed company statutes if you are starting a company

This is a thorough list, but it's always possible that there will be changes or additions. Cross-reference the list provided here and in each visa type's section with the definitive list will provided by your consulate or préfecture.

Accompanying Family Members

Generally speaking, visa applicants have the right to bring their minor children (except for programs like TAPIF, FACC, and Work Holiday, which specifically prohibit it) and their spouses to France with them. However, these accompanying family members will usually have the status of "visitor" unless they meet the criteria for other visa types and submit successful applications. Bringing other family members (elderly parents, siblings, adult children) will require the applicant to apply for a long stay "visitor" visa. The family members already residing in France can provide proof that they will provide financial support, lodging, and assistance with the application, but it will not help the applicant to get another status.

One of the advantages of the Passeport Talents visas is that the spouse of a PT visa holder will get a "PT trailing partner" visa, which enables the accompanying spouse to work. In some ways, this visa is even more advantageous than the initial PT visa, because it is similar to a Vie Privée et Familiale visa in that the family member is entitled to work, in any profession and with any status. This means that the Passeport Talents visa holder is restricted in employment to the original visa (tied to the salaried position, or business, or artistic proposal), but the spouse is not, and can choose to find a CDD or CDI, work part time or full time, or become an autoentrepreneur or start her own business.

In most other cases, the spouse will get a visitor visa, which does not allow them to work. They will have to provide all of the same documents for the visitor visa and show proof of financial resources in order to get their own visa. Financial resources can include the spouse's projected salary or income upon arrival, based on a work contract or business plan.

Bringing Minor Children

If you would like to bring your minor children to France, the process is very easy. You will have to apply for visas for them individually at the VFS office or local French consulate, which involves making appointments for them along with you, and paying the appointment fee.

Technically, some consulates advise that minor children under 12 do not have to appear in person; however, I recommend bringing all children with you to the visa appointment. Older children will have to be fingerprinted as part of the process.

Minor children require their own complete visa applications, including a long-stay visa form completed on the France-Visas website. There is a section on the long-stay visa application form where you can list family members who are accompanying you, as well as their relationship to you. Each form should list all family members in the group. They will also require their own passport, where a visa will be affixed, passport photos, and a birth certificate. If your children are young, you should ideally have these photos taken at a studio with an experienced photographer, so they are not rejected.

If you are not relocating with a partner, you will have to show some kind of document showing full legal custody and decision-making ability for the children. This could take the form of the other parent's death certificate, if deceased, notarized authorization from the non-custodial parent, documents showing the other parent has relinquished their rights, or court documents showing full custody.

Work

While it is extremely rare for minors to work in France due to strict labor laws, it is technically possible. If both parents are foreigners, the child's work authorization will depend on the parent's ability to work. For example, there are often casting calls for child models or for bilingual children to appear in films or television. The child would only be able to participate in such a project if at least one of the parents has the ability to work in France. If the parents have visitor visas, the child would not be eligible to work on the project.

Documents to Provide for Minor Child's Visa Application

- ☑ Long-stay visa application for each child, listing all family members traveling together
- ☑ Passport
- ☑ Passport photos
- ☑ Birth certificate
- ☑ Livret de famille, if applicable (French families)
- ☑ Proof of custody or authorization from the second parent (if not relocating and applying together)

DCEM - Document de Circulation de l'Etranger Mineur

Minors residing in France do not need to go through the OFII procedure until they are 18; however, they do need a document called a DCEM to show that they live in France. You will need this document when you travel with your children back and forth to the EU, to present along with your passports and cartes de séjour to prove that they reside with you.

The DCEM can be obtained at your local prefecture and is valid for 5 years. You will have to apply individually for each child after completing the OFII procedure and provide your passport, visa, proof of residence, and children's birth certificates along with French-sized passport photos taken in a Photomaton machine. If you are the only parent, they may require proof of sole custody (translated into French) to be able to issue the document, as both parents have to approve it. Typically, procedure is that one parent has to appear to drop off the request, and the other parent has to appear to pick up the documents. The children also have to appear in-person for pickup.

Documents to Provide for DCEM
- ☑ DCEM application form, available at the préfecture
- ☑ Parent's passport, visa, & OFII stamp
- ☑ Child's passport
- ☑ Passport photos
- ☑ Birth certificate
- ☑ Livret de famille, if applicable (French families)
- ☑ Proof of custody or authorization from the second parent

When Children Turn 18
Minor children who are born in France to foreign parents are not French at birth (there is no *jus solis* citizenship) can obtain French nationality automatically before age 18 simply by requesting it. Minor children whose parent(s) obtain French nationality are automatically naturalized along with their parent(s). Only one parent has to be a French citizen for the children to become French.

For minor children residing in France with foreign parents, but who were not born in France, they will have to complete the OFII process and obtain their own titres de séjour once they turn 18.

If they have been living in France and completely educated in France since they were small children, they can have the opportunity to apply for naturalization as teenagers. It is VERY IMPORTANT that they complete immigration and naturalization procedures at the right time, and before leaving France to pursue education abroad. Otherwise, they risk having to start the immigration procedures from the beginning as adults, as if they had never resided in France.

In a particularly unfortunate situation, I once had a young man contact me who had been living with his family in France since he was a young child. Upon adulthood, his mother and sister had been naturalized, but he had not. During his studies, he became depressed and dropped out of his program, losing his "student" visa and his legal status in France while he recovered.

As your children approach adulthood, it is important that they understand what they will need to do if they want to continue live in France, to avoid a situation where they lose their status and have to leave a home they've known since childhood.

Bringing Adult Children

If you have children over age 18 who would like to accompany you to France, they will have to apply for their own visa individually, and they will be treated as adults. They will need to choose the visa type from this book that is most appropriate and meet all of the requirements on their own. Of course, if you are providing financial support, they could get a student or visitor visa relatively easily, especially if you attest that they will be living with you. Likewise, they will have to complete their own administrative procedures upon arrival, including the OFII visit and renewals at the prefecture.

Regroupement Familial

People who have been residing regularly in France for more than 18 months can bring family members over to live with them through a process called Regroupement Familial. There are a few different ways in which this procedure might be appropriate, such as if a person living in France married someone back in their home country and wanted to bring over their spouse. Two foreign nationals from different countries who reside and marry in France can also go through a process called "regroupement familial sur place," which ensures that they maintain the right to remain in France together.

This process is started through the mairie (town hall) where the French resident lives, and requires a few administrative procedures, such as ensuring the resident's apartment is big enough for the arriving family members and that their financial resources are sufficient to support the whole family.

Using the France-Visas Website

In order to apply for your French visa, you will have to create a long-stay visa application on the France Visas website. After creating an account, you can create several visa applications for all members of your family, indicating the visa type you are applying for, the length of your stay, and all personal information about you and your family.

The form is relatively straightforward, but there are a few glitches and tricks you should be aware of.

Create a separate long-stay visa application for each member of your party, including children. Technically, children under 12 do not have to be physically present for the visa appointment, but it's a good idea to bring them anyway if you can.

Every time you make edits to a form, the length of your stay may default back to < 3 months. Make sure you fix it every time and that when you finalize the complete application, it shows the full length of your stay, or > 12 months.

Do not indicate a stay shorter than 12 months if you would like a renewable visa. In fact, explicitly state in your cover letter that you are planning on staying for 2 years or longer, so you receive a renewable visa. Some consulates will default to nonrenewable visas if you do not specify.

Indicate all accompanying members of your family.

For relatives in France, only list immediate family (parents, children, or siblings) who already live in France. You do not need to list everyone you know or a random cousin.

Do not list a partner as family if you are not engaged or planning to be married within the next few months. If they suspect you are going to France to marry someone, they will want you to apply for a "vie privée" visa or for "regroupement familial."

It is perfectly acceptable to have accommodations in a rented apartment, AirBnb, or friend's home for a month or so while you look for permanent accommodation. List the name and address of where you will be staying, along with "rented apartment" or the name of the person who will be hosting you. You no longer have to provide proof of accommodation for any particular length of time.

Your "financial resources" and "means of support" should be solely related to your reason for going to France. If you are going for a salaried position, it should be "income from this job and savings." If you are going for a freelance visa, it should be "freelance income and personal savings." If you are going for a student visa, it should be "personal savings and support from parents/financial guarantor." You should not indicate a job as a source of income unless you are specifically seeking a visa for that job.

Reference one specific location as where you intend to stay. If you intend to travel within France or move around, you should still have a home base with a rented address that will remain constant throughout your time in France. Otherwise, you will be considered a tourist and will get a temporary stay visa.

Create your long-stay visa application here: https://france-visas.gouv.fr

Where to Apply

You can apply for a French visa in your country of residence. In most cases, this is going to be your home country or country of nationality. If you live in a third country, you can apply at the local French consulate if you have proof of residence there. For example, an American citizen living in the UK can apply for a French visa at the French consulate in London, assuming she has a UK residency permit. An Indian citizen living in the US can apply for a visa in the US by showing a valid green card (but usually not a student visa).

As of 2019, Americans can apply for a French visa at any VFS Global office in the US. Likewise, Canadians can apply for a French visa at any VFS Global office in Canada. Applicants are no longer restricted to submitting their applications at the consulate or VFS office for their region.

To find your local French consulate or VFS office, you can locate your country on this map: https://france-visas.gouv.fr/fr_FR/web/us/a-qui-sadresser

You will be taken to a contact page for your country's consulates and VFS Global offices, with links to make an appointment.

Making an Appointment

You can find the appointment page for your country by finding your local consulate or VFS office using the link above, and clicking on the "Prendre Rendez-Vous" button next to your local consulate's contact information.

To make an appointment with VFS Global, you can create an account here: https://online.vfsglobal.com/Global-Appointment/Account/RegisteredLogin

By clicking on the "Create New User" underneath the login box, and registering a new account.

You can use this account to make multiple visa appointments together for people in your group, and paying the fee online. If you create a group with multiple people, you can schedule all of your appointments together. Each member of the group traveling must have their own appointment, pay the fee, and be physically present at the time of submission.

The fee for an appointment is around $30, paid in your local currency. This does not include the visa processing fee, which is charged by the French consulate and is indicated separately for each visa type in its checklist. You will have to pay this fee online in order to schedule the appointment.

You can reschedule your visa appointment up to 48 hours

prior to the appointment and choose a new time at no additional charge. If you try to reschedule less than 48 hours in advance, or if you do not show up to your scheduled appointment, you will have to pay the fee again to schedule a new appointment.

Typically, new appointment times become available between the 15th-20th of the month for the following month. During peak times (late spring and summer), it can be difficult to find an available appointment time, so start the reservation process early and check back regularly. Each visa center sets its own appointment times and releases new appointment slots on their own schedule.

Pro tip: Sometimes, after registering as a new user with VFS, the login page doesn't work properly and tries to redirect you to selecting your home country and destination country. This is a glitch that has still not been fixed after over a year fo visa processing. To get around the issue, try going to the France-visas's 'A qui s'adresser?" page (here: https://france-visas.gouv.fr/fr_FR/web/us/a-qui-sadresser), finding your consulate in the directory, and clicking the "Book an Appointment" button. For some reason, this method tends to redirect you to the correct page and enables logging into VFS.

Timeline for Applying

You can apply for your visa up to 90 days before you wish to arrive in France, or 90 days before the start of your program if you are enrolling in studies. If you have to travel to another city for your visa appointment, you should consider when it will be most convenient for you to travel.

Depending on the consulate or VFS Global office, new visa appointments become available 4-6 weeks in advance. At certain times of year (like winter), you will have no trouble finding an appointment for the next day or the next week. From April through September, however, it can be more difficult to secure an application, and you should plan to do so as soon as the appointments for that month open up. This can involve creating an account and logging in regularly to check appointment availability.

If you are scheduling your visa appointment in advance, remember to factor in things like waiting for CampusFrance approval (3 weeks for standard, 3 business days for rushed) or DIRECCTE approval of work contracts (8 weeks) plus a bit of a buffer between when you submit all of your information and when you can expect to receive your approval for your visa appointment.

Once you apply, it typically takes 10-14 calendar days to receive your passport back with your visa stamped inside. However, I recommend to my clients that they apply for their visa no later than 1 month before their scheduled departure to ensure they get their passports back on time. This is especially important if there are French holidays or holidays in the country where you are applying, or if you are applying during the spring and summer when more applications are processed.

Student visas: you will have to wait 3 weeks for CampusFrance validation, OR pay a $150 rush fee for confirmation within 3 business days. If you are *already* accepted to a university or language program, we can complete the CF process and visa application documents in 7-10 days. If you are applying to a language program and are *not* accepted yet, expect it to take 14-21 days from choosing a language school and paying the deposit to submitting CampusFrance documents. If you are applying to university programs, the application process will take around 3 months. Note that not all countries have to go through CampusFrance first. Citizens of the United States, and most of Asia, South America, and Africa have to go through CampusFrance, while nationals of Canada, Australia, and New Zealand are notably exempt from this procedure.

Visitor and family visas: Allow 7-10 days to gather documents and prepare the application, but these can be done relatively quickly.

Profession libérale and commerçant visa: Allow 6-8 weeks to write the business plan and do the financial projections. A good rule of thumb is that the more easily you can get letters of support and collaboration, and the clearer your idea for your business, the faster you're going to be able to put everything together. If you are starting a brand-new business, you may want to take up to 12 weeks so you can hammer out all of the details of your business.

Passeport talents entrepreneur visa: These are approved by a committee, require a €30.000 investment in starting a French business, and are subject to A LOT more scrutiny than the "profession libérale" visa in terms of viability and planning. Therefore, expect these applications to take about 12-16 weeks to prepare and 3 months to review.

The Visa Application Submission Process

Once you have made a visa appointment with your local French consulate or VFS Global office, you will physically go to your appointment and bring the required documents.

At the designated appointment time, the VFS official will take your official document checklist, provided with your visa application form from the FranceVisas website, and ask you to submit each document on the list, along with your photos and your passport.

The VFS offices typically have a photo booth as well as photocopying and printing services available for an additional fee. They may also have prepaid mailling envelopes available for returning your passport(s). Please fill out the mailing envelope with the address where you will be staying prior to your departure for France.

The VFS official you interact with has basically no authority over your application and can't answer any questions about what the French embassy will approve. Their job is to verify that you submit what's on the list, that your insurance policy meets certain requirements, and to pass it on to the French embassy, which makes the decision and issues the visa. So, it is fairly useless to argue with the VFS official about the list or to try to get information from them about your submission.

The VFS office will not take any original documents, but

will only take photocopies. They will, however, take your original passport, and take your fingerprints. Each day, VFS sends all of the visa applications overnight to the French Embassy in Washington, DC, where they are processed before being returned to you.

Estimated Visa Processing Time

The French embassy advises that visa processing can take 21 business days after your visa appointment. For this reason, I typically advise my clients to schedule their visa appointment no later than 1 month before their intended departure date.

The vast majority of my clients get their passports returned to them, with visas inside, within 7-10 calendar days of their appointment. It may take a couple of extra days if the embassy emails you to request additional documents (see below). Longer processing times usually only happen if you are not a citizen of the country where you are applying (e.g. a Mexican citizen with a green card residing and applying in the US) or if you are from a list of countries that requires additional processing checks.

Requesting Additional Information

Check your email regularly, as the French embassy may contact you by email for additional information abut your application. For example, if your visa insurance policy doesn't meet the requirements or the policy's proof of coverage letter doesn't provide all of the required information, they will contact you to ask for an updated policy. Similarly, if they feel that you don't have enough money in your bank account, they will ask for additional proof of funds. You should send the documents they request as soon as possible, as failing to provide the information within 7 calendar days could lead to your visa application being returned, unprocessed.

I tell my clients that if the French embassy asks for additional information, it's a good sign. It means they are ready to issue the visa on the merits of your application, and the information you send back will enable them to check their last box and to proceed with finalizing your visa. After all, if they were going to reject you, they would have just sent back your passport with a rejection letter.

What if you don't have a document?

To make the process as painless and as smooth as possible, you should go to your appointment prepared with every document on your checklist, and inquire before the appointment if there are any documents you're not sure about or aren't sure how to get. However, sometimes the information you get prior to the appointment is incomplete.

If the document list appears to be wrong, and you don't have something they say you need, write an attestation on a blank piece of paper explaining why you don't have the document, to include with your file. In one memorable situation, a client was held up at the VFS office in Los Angeles because the France-Visas document list was wrong. She was applying for a visa as a freelancer (profession libérale) and despite having checked off the correct boxes on the long-stay visa form, her document list included items for someone starting a business, like company formation documents.

She messaged me because the VFS official was going to mark her application "incomplete" since she hadn't provided these documents she didn't need! I quickly wrote an attestation in French identifying the documents she didn't have, explained why they weren't needed for her proposed business structure, and indicated that the list included them in error. I emailed it to her, and the VFS official included the document with the rest of her application. She successfully got her correct visa type.

Getting Status Updates on Your Application

You can log into the VFS website for updates on your visa's status to know when it has been received by the French embassy, when it is processing, and when it will be returned to you.

Common Reasons for Visa Rejections

The last time I checked the statistics, I learned that around 3.8 million requests for French visas were processed by French embassies and consulates around the world during a single calendar year. Around 300,000 visas of all types were issued. The French consulates make determinations about who gets a visa and who does not based on several factors: your income, your credentials, what your stated purpose is in requesting the visa, and how likely they think you are to violate the terms of your visa by doing something you're not supposed to do.

Your job, in assembling the visa application, is to paint a clear picture of exactly who you are, where your money is going to come from, and what you will contribute to France by being here. You want to show exactly what you will be doing with your time and ensure that all of your stated plans fit neatly into one of the "boxes" we've outlined in this book.

France is not a place where having lots of different simultaneous projects and stepping outside the box is appreciated. If they don't understand what it is you want to do when they are reviewing your visa, your chances of getting that visa are not good. Conversely, if you present a clear and compelling case for one visa type and the documents you provide give sufficient supporting evidence for your claims, you're very likely to be approved.

Channel your inner ADA Alex Cabot from watching all of those old Law & Order SVU reruns (she's my absolute fave) and put together a visa application like you are putting together a court case. You have no obligation to turn over exculpatory evidence that can torpedo your "case," so focus on the facts and build your case narrowly. Include only what needs to be included, nothing more. No unnecessary explaining.

Don't speculate about what you could do or what you might do. Don't equivocate. Don't give them ammunition to look for a reason to reject you. Don't lie by omission, but don't be overly forthcoming about your motivations. The more information you give them, the more information they have to process and analyze before issuing your visa.

Include in your visa application only that which can be proved with supporting documentation and that which shows a well-thought-out plan for what you will do upon arrival.

Here are some of the most common reasons I've seen for visa rejections.

1. **Being unclear in your intent.**
If you apply for a visa and do not present a plan for what you are going to do while on that visa, and how it will impact your life, you may end up with a rejection or a visa you don't want, like the long séjour temporaire. Equivocating or being ambivalent about what you're going

to do once you arrive in France, or being unsure of the future you are creating, or trying to tell the French consulate what you think they want to hear will not work.

Certain clients have expressed to me that their initial visa applications were rejected or approved as LST visa because they didn't want to seem too sure of themselves in planning to stay in France for multiple years. The resulting miscommunication meant they'd have to go through the additional expense and process of returning to their home country to get the new visa. If your plan is to stay for multiple years in France, it's okay – and encouraged – to say so. Project yourself into the future. What is the next few years going to look like for you? If you're a student or an au pair, what are the academic programs you might do *after* those initial programs end? If you're doing a work contract, how will the job help to build your career and insinuate you into your field and networking opportunities in France?

Be clear on how moving to France impacts your life plan and how this visa enhances that plan.

2. Saying you're going to work (but you're not applying for a work visa).

Indicating on your visa application that you plan to work, seek employment, or be self-employed while you're not applying for a work visa is a sure way to get your visa application rejected. This seems to be most common with students, who put that they plan to support themselves on cash savings and find a babysitting or part-time job upon arrival. While the student visa technically allows its bearers to work part-time, working should not be a motivation for requesting the visa.

Similarly, applying for a visitor visa and indicating that you plan to work remotely or run a business remotely can lead to rejection. Referencing any type of work on your visa application other than work specifically linked to your visa is a bad idea. If your visa application is rejected for this reason, it will be impossible for you to prove that you have decided *not* to plan to work in France or to seek employment upon arrival. You will have to wait even longer to reapply for a new visa.

3. Saying you're going to be with a romantic partner.

If your relationship is serious enough for you to be moving to a new country to be with someone, it's serious enough to make things official, through marriage. At least, that's how the consulate will see it.

A common issue I see is people applying for student or visitor visas to move to France and "test out" the relationship with a previously long-distance significant other. They aren't ready to get married, and so look to other visa types that would enable them to live in France.

The problem arises when the partner is going to potentially be a source of income (financial guarantee) or of housing.

If you have none of your own financial resources and plan on relying on someone to whom you are not legally attached, you are risking major problems should anything happen in your relationship. A romantic partner who is not legally bound to you has no obligation to provide you with anything. Abusive situations aside, you would be completely stranded without a job, without money, and without a place to live if things didn't work out for whatever reason. Don't put yourself in that situation. The consulate won't allow you to.

4. Saying you're looking for a job.

Applying for a visitor visa to work remotely or to look for jobs with the intention of switching visa statuses is also a no-no. You should expect to maintain the same visa status for at least two years before switching, and any indication that you do not intend to maintain the status you are applying for will result in your application being rejected.

If you do come to France with a particular visa type and the intention of finding a job, keep that out of your initial visa application, as actually *getting* a job is merely speculative. When you actually find a job, you will have to return to your home country to apply for a new visa unless you have already been in France for more than a year and renewed your visa once.

5. Not having your docs in order.

Since the VFS takeover of the French visa application procedures in 2018, there have been lots of problems with visas being misprocessed, the wrong visa types being awarded, or long delays. Part of the problem was that the VFS bureaucrats were not familiar with the different French visa types or the documents required for them, and in some cases, they weren't requesting everything they really needed for the French embassy to process the requests. It doesn't help that the France-Visas site doesn't give you a list of required documents until AFTER you complete and finalize your visa application, meaning that you can't get the list and begin assembling your file until you've already completed a long-stay visa form. The information and document lists have been completely removed from the websites of French consulates in the US, and other countries' visa information is outdated or different. And anyone who did their visa application more than a year ago and who does not have experience with the process in several locations is not a good source of information.

Moral of the story: bring ALL of your documents, and even the ones you don't think you need. I've provided complete checklists in this book for each visa type, and you should bring things that aren't on the official list and even documents you don't think you need. Having more documents that you can pull out of your binder if they ask is better than not having them and having to send something in or book a new appointment.

And, make sure they take all of the documents you've prepared, even if they don't ask for them or they aren't officially required. Cover letters, project plans, extra bank statements, the works.

6. Applying for wrong visa type for what you want to do.

It should go without saying, but applying for a visa you're not fully qualified for and don't have adequate proof for will very likely result in a rejection. There is not a lot of wiggle room in French visa applications, and the requirements are the *minimum* to get you a visa. You can certainly meet all of the requirements and still be rejected, so don't apply for a visa you're not eligible for. It will simply be a black mark on your file and can be held against you if you reapply for a different visa type within a short period of time.

Again, you should narrowly construe your visa application for the specific thing you're applying to do, and avoid referencing any personal projects or ideas that do *not* fit that plan.

7. Not having enough money or a high enough salary.

If you do not have enough personal cash resources to meet the minimum requirements for your visa or will not earn enough doing whatever job you plan to do in France, you will not get the visa. Ensure that you have at least the minimum cash requirement for your visa type and can show at least 3 bank statements with those amounts. Do not rely on someone outside of your family for income or support, and do not plan to provide a financial guarantor for visa types other than student or visitor.

Rejections, New Applications & Appeals

The French consulate does not have to give you a reason for rejecting your visa application unless you are applying as the family member of a French citizen. It can therefore be quite difficult to ascertain the reasons for the rejection and to submit a new application. If your application is rejected, you have the option of submitting a new application, or of submitting an appeal. Of course, the best way to ensure your visa application is accepted is to consult a professional *before* you submit it, to ensure no red flags are raised and that all conditions for the visa application are met. It is far easier to avoid rejection in the first place than it is to modify and resubmit a failed application.

Sometimes, there is no real reason for your rejection, other than the fact that they reject a certain number of applications and yours may not have made the cut that day.

A new application is the easiest and fastest solution, because you can submit a new application as soon as you can get a new appointment. There is no waiting period for when you can try again. However, in order to be successful the second time, you have to know what, if anything, was wrong with your application in the first place. Sometimes, it's a simple procedural error, or not providing enough supporting documents. Other times, it's a bell that is very hard to unring, like stating you are going to work or look for a job, when you shouldn't be. If you put on one application that you plan to find employment, how do you *disprove* that you're going to be job hunting on the next application?

If you are able to travel to France on just your passport and are going for studies or on a visitor visa (not to work), you may consider going for up to 90 days as a tourist, and then returning several months later to apply for a new visa. Obviously, you would not be able to work or start a planned job on the "tourist" status. Having a cool-down period before submitting a new application and taking the time to make the application more focused can help to ensure approval the second time around.

Another option is to file a "recours," or an appeal, with the Ministry of the Interior. This process involves sending your complete file, along with all supporting documents, to Nantes for processing. I do not recommend doing this without having a professional examine your file and helping you to prepare a new application and then the appeal, because 90% of rejections are upheld while only about 10% are overturned. The process can take up to 8 weeks to get a reply, and then you will still have to submit a new application through the local French consulate or VFS office.

Arriving in France

Your visa will be issued with the start date you've requested, and once your passport has your visa in it, it will be mailed back to you or be sent back to the VFS office for pick-up.

Once you arrive in France with your VLS-TS, you will have to validate your visa through OFII, the Office Français d'Immigration et d'Intégration. This section describes the updated OFII procedure that was 'dématérialisé', or digitalized, as of February 2019. You will need to complete the OFII registration procedures in order to renew your visa at the end of the first year.

You must complete the OFII procedures within 90 days of arriving in France. Ideally, you will submit your OFII registration very soon after arrival and have all of your OFII appointments before this 90 day period is over. If not, don't worry too much. As long as you submit the OFII registration within the 90 days, you should be fine. The great thing is that the new online procedure should prevent registrations from being lost and misplaced, which sometimes happened when everything was done on paper.

1. Find Housing.

In order to complete the OFII process online, you will have to have an address where you can send and receive mail. This will ideally be your permanent address for your whole year in France. If you have reseved temporary housing upon arrival, you should spend your first few weeks seeking a permanent place to live, and only register with OFII once you have found a longer lease. You will have to enter your address on the form, and provide a "justificatif de domiclie" in the form of rent receipts, apartment insurance, an electricity bill, or an attestation d'hébérgement from your landlord.

Alternatively, if you have friends who live in the same region where you are located, you may ask them to use their address for the initial OFII registration. This allows you to begin the process earlier while you are still looking for your housing. If you find permanent housing in the meantime, you can change your official address at your OFII appointment by providing a "justificatif de domicile" in your name; otherwise, you can continue to use their address by providing an attestation d'hébérgement from your friends at your appointment, and then changing your address once you sign a longer lease or renew your carte de séjour. Normally, you will not receive any mail from OFII or from anyone; they will invite you to your appointments by email.

2. Purchase a timbre fiscal dématérialisé.

A timbre fiscal is a stamp you purchase to pay taxes on certain services from the préfecture. You will most likely only use these for your OFII visit and your titre de séjour renewals at the préfecture.

The timbre fiscal for the OFII procedure can be purchased online right on the website where you complete the OFII procedure. You will need to have a credit or debit card available.

Go to https://administration-etrangers-en-france.interieur.gouv.fr/particuliers/#/ and click on the tab for "Acheter un timbre fiscal." You will have to select the amount of the stamp you need to purchase.

If you do not know for sure what amount you should buy, you will need to begin filling out the OFII form first, as it will tell you once you've begun to input your information. You should verify the amount before purchasing the stamp, as you cannot buy multiple stamps for the same OFII form.

After clicking through to purchase the stamp in the correct amount, you will download a document to receive a 16-digit code, which you will input into the last page of the OFII form. Write down the code or save it as a PDF for the next step.

3. Complete the Online OFII Form.

You will need your passport with your long-stay visa, your date of arrival in France, and the address where you are staying for this step. You can open up a second tab to begin this procedure at the same time as you purchase the timbre fiscal, since beginning the OFII form will enable you to learn the exact amount you have to pay. The amount varies based on the visa type.

On this page (https://administration-etrangers-en-france.interieur.gouv.fr/particuliers/#/), you will have to put in your name, visa number (on the top right corner of your visa), its start date, request date, arrival date, and various personal information. You will also have to identify the visa type that you received, at which point you will learn the price of your timbre fiscal. Complete the purchase of the timbre in a separate window, and enter the 16-digit code from the timbre fiscal to pay and complete the procedure.

Once you have entered all of the information and submitted the page, save it to PDF to keep evidence of your submission.

4. Receive Your Convocation(s).

It will take several weeks for OFII to get back to you, but you will receive a convocation by email inviting you to one or two visits at the OFII office (depending on your visa type), and you will receive a separate convocation for each. Along with the convocation, OFII will provide a list of documents that you will need to bring along with your visa in order to validate it. Aside from your passport with visa, passport photos, and a justificatif de domicile less than 3 months old, you should expect to bring documents related to your visa type: business registration, proof of enrollment in your academic program, signed work contract and payslips, or other documents as they fit your situation.

If you do not receive a response from OFII within 6 weeks, you can try calling or emailing your OFII office at (city where your OFII office is located)@ofii.fr. You can also try going in person if you are close. If you opt to go in-person, avoid peak times like 9:00, 10:30, 1:30, or 15:00 when most appointments are scheduled. Try to go halfway between those peak hours. Some OFII offices have scheduled walk-in hours for people to ask questions and get information without an appointment. Check your local OFII office's website for details.

5. *Go to Your OFII Visits.*

Show up to the appropriate OFII office on the date and time indicated. Arrive 15-20 minutes early if possible, as arriving earlier will mean you will get an earlier ticket and get out of there faster.

Everyone will get a convocation for a medical visit, which is a very basic exam where they test your vision and hearing, X-ray your chest for tuberculosis, and ask about your vaccinations. If you have a record of your vaccines, bring it if possible. For the X-ray, you will have to undress from the waist up, so ladies, bring a scarf to cover yourself on the brief walk from the changing stall to the x-ray machine, and wear pants and a t-shirt so you only have to take off your shirt and bra.

Those on a work visa or who have married a French citizen will also be invited to an "integration" day, where you will take a French language test to see if you are eligible for free or reduced-priced French classes through the local mairie. You will also learn about living in France and respecting French values. You will learn a bit about French administration and how things work in France, and you will also learn about your rights while you live here. Part of the program is designed to acclimate immigrants from non-Western cultures whose cultural practices may not be compatible with French laws about human rights, such as polygamy or preventing a wife from leaving the house or forcing her to wear a niqab. Take it in stride; there's no exam, and once it's done, it's done forever.

Once you have completed your required visits, you will be asked to present your attestation of attendance at each one, along with the documents you were asked to bring. The OFII agents will put a sticker in your passport to officially validate your visa, and this sticker, or "vignette," will serve as your first official Titre de Séjour. Make a photocopy of it as soon as you can, along with a photocopy of your visa and passport's ID page, and save them in multiple places - on your phone, in your email, in the cloud. If you ever lose your passport or if you are walking around without your passport and are asked to present ID, it could come in handy. And you will replace the passport, visa, and vignette much more quickly if you have copies.

6. *If You MUST Miss an OFII Visit.*

First of all, don't. You should be there on the days they invite you in, no matter how inconvenient it will be. Rearrange your schedule if you must.

If you absolutely, positively, 100% cannot make one of the appointment times, go to what you can. (Sometimes the two appointments will be scheduled together; other times they will be a few days apart.) Once you have missed the appointment(s), email the OFII office or go in person to reschedule. Going in-person is preferable, as they may not respond or reschedule you over email. Bring your passport and old convocation so they can easily look you up in their system.

DO NOT MISS THE SECOND APPOINTMENT. If you miss the appointment once, they will reschedule you once without too much of an issue. Miss the second appointment, and they are very likely to tell you that you're out of luck, and that you will have to go back home for a new visa at the end of the year.

You will not be able to renew your visa without completing the OFII validation process.

7. Keep Your Documentation.

You will receive an attestation for having completed your OFII medical and integration visits. You should scan these documents and keep them in a safe place with photocopies of everything to ensure you have them for your renewal. You will have to provide a copy of these attestations the first time you renew your visa, but not any of the subsequent times.

Once you renew, the préfecture will keep a record of which visit(s) you've done. If you're a student, you will only be required to do the medical visit, but if you then change your visa type to salarié, for example, you will get another convocation to do the integration visit as well. If you haven't done one of the required visits for your new visa type, you may have to complete it before they will give you your new visa status.

8. Set a Reminder to Renew Your Visa.

You will need to make an appointment to renew your visa about 90 days before it expires. Set a reminder in your Google calendar or on your phone for 90 days before your visa's expiration date, so you can begin looking into how to make an appointment to renew and gathering your documents.

Renewing Your Visa

If you receive a "VLS-TS", or a "Visa Long Séjour valant Titre de Séjour" and validate your visa via the OFII process upon arrival in France, you can renew the same visa status at the end of your first year directly in France provided that you continue to meet the conditions for maintaining your visa.

In this section, we will discuss how to renew your visa if you are keeping the SAME visa type. You will need to renew your initial visa status at least once before you can switch to another visa status, unless there are exceptional circumstances. (And even with exceptional circumstances, you better write a good cover letter explaining what they are on your change of status application.)

Note that if you receive a "Long Séjour Temporaire" visa and you are "dispensé" (exempt) from the OFII procedure, you will not be able to renew your visa or change your visa status. Even if you do the OFII procedure (which is required for all work visa types), you cannot renew a non-renewable visa type such as "work holiday" or "salarié en mission" for example.

The renewal process is managed at the préfecture for each region, and can vary slightly between regions depending on the different systems they put in place to manage applicants. In some préfectures, you can make an appointment online through a web portal and receive a convocation by email or download. In other préfectures, you must go to the préfecture and line up to make an appointment, sometimes very early in the morning. In still other préfectures, you submit your details online via a contact form, and the préfecture responds several days or weeks later with an appointment for you.

When to Make Your Renewal Appointment

You can make your appointment to renew your titre de séjour up to 90 days before your current titre de séjour is set to expire. Some préfectures advise that you make your appointment even farther in advance because there is so much demand, but usually this isn't necessary.

If you're going to need to travel shortly after you renew your titre de séjour, you can make your appointment farther in advance to have your appointment earlier (before your titre de séjour expires). Alternatively, you can make your appointment *closer* to your titre de séjour's expiration date, such that your renewal appointment is several weeks AFTER your current titre de séjour expires.

It is 100% OKAY if your renewal appointment is AFTER your titre de séjour expires. DON'T WORRY. It happens all the time and is totally normal, even if you make the appointment when you're supposed to. As long as the date you make the appointment is before your titre de séjour expires, you won't have any issues with your renewal.

(In fact, it used to be much worse - people would have their renewal appointments months after their cards expired, and would not be issued the new 1-year carte de séjour until it was almost expired. They'd have to make appointments to renew immediately upon receiving the new near-expired card, and the cycle would begin again. Fortunately, France has mostly moved past those days due to a few changes in legislation and how the cards are processed and produced.)

There can be some advantages to having your renewal appointment several weeks later than you are supposed to make it. For example, a client of mine who is a tour guide on a "profession libérale" status arrived in May, but the bulk of her activity and income are during the summer months. Taking a day off for an appointment in May or early June would mean she'd miss out on income for the day of her appointment, and she'd have little time to prepare when she's working. It also means that her most recent months of income are relatively low compared to what she's capable of making during the height of tourist season in the summer. If she makes her appointment in February and has her appointment in May, her file won't look quite as good as if she makes an appointment in early May for August or September. By having her appointment a couple of months after she is "supposed" to, she'll have higher income to show in her most recent months, and has leverage for requesting a multi-year carte de séjour.

Scheduling Your Appointment

Once you've decided approximately when you'd like to have your visa appointment, you have a few options for scheduling depending on your department. You will have to learn about your specific department's renewal procedures and how to make an appointment by googling the city where your préfecture is, + "prise de rendez-vous renouvellement titre de séjour." You can also go to your préfecture for information or ask other expats in your region. As always, do not rely on outdated information from those who have not renewed recently, don't have your visa type, or are in a different region from you.

Online: Some préfectures have the option of scheduling your appointment directly online. The Paris préfecture, for example, allows this. You will need to log into the appointment calendar with your AGDEF number (see the next section), your full name, and the expiration date, and will have access to an appointment calendar so you can choose your own date and time.

The website for Paris renewals is https://www.prefecturedepolice.interieur.gouv.fr/Demarches/Services-en-ligne/Pour-vous-aider/Toutes-les-prises-de-rendez-vous.

By Email: Some préfectures have a contact form on their website which you complete and submit to get an appointment. In this case, you will have to include all of your contact details and visa information, and the préfecture will respond within several weeks to give you an appointment. This usually means you cannot select the date and time, and if you get a date that is impossible for you to attend, you will have to start the process over.

By Phone: You can call 3430 and pay €0.06 per minute to make your appointment by phone. The operator will take your contact details and propose several appointment dates. You will not have much choice in what they offer, so if it isn't at the right time, you'll have to call back on another day. After verifying your email address, you will receive your convocation by email within 72 hours of your call.

In Person: Obviously this is the most inconvenient way to make an appointment, as it usually requires going very early in the morning and waiting in line for several hours to get a ticket, and then waiting for several hours in the waiting room to be called. In some cases, you do not make an appointment for a renewal and simply show up in-person with your complete file to renew. Check whether this is the case for your préfecture. (Lyon is like this for some visa types.) Even if you do not expect them to take your file on the same day, you should bring your passport and titre de séjour, justificatif de domicile, and photos, along with any other document you already have for your renewal, such as proof of attendance and grades if you're a student. Some préfectures will use the appointment making process to ensure that your application is complete and to go over anything you're missing before they will schedule your appointment.

By Mail: Some préfectures have you submit your complete renewal application by mail, send your récipissé back by mail, and you only have to be physically present to pick up your card. If this is the case for your préfecture, make sure you send your complete renewal packet no later than 60 days before your titre de séjour expires, and send it by lettre recommandé avec accusé de réception (certified mail with delivery receipt) to confirm they have received it and to provide proof in case it's ever needed. You should send copies of all of your documents, not originals, if you have to make an appointment in this way. (Versailles and Bordeaux are like this for some visa types.)

Information You'll Need to Schedule

Your AGDREF number: This is a 10-digit number, usually starting with 99, that is listed on the side of your carte de séjour or on your OFII vignette in your passport. AGDREF stands for "Application de Gestion des Dossiers des Ressortissants Etrangers en France" and it will be your ID number of sorts while you are living in France. You will keep the same AGDREF number even if you switch visa statuses, and it will follow you until you are naturalized. (Or until you return to your home country to get a new visa type and start over with a new AGDREF number.)

Your Full Name: You will need to input your complete name, including all middle names, into the online form. If the form doesn't work for whatever reason, ensure that you are typing all of your names exactly as they appear on the

Your Visa's Expiration Date: This will be listed on your initial visa, or on your titre de séjour. Remember that the date is listed day-month-year.

After Scheduling

Once your appointment is scheduled, you should receive a Convocation. A Convocation is an official document showing the date and time of your appointment and where you should present yourself on that day. You will need it, along with your passport and titre de séjour and all supporting documents, to access the préfecture and the appointment windows.

If you are not traveling, your titre de séjour (even if it's expired) and your convocation are enough to prove that you can legally stay in France. If you do not plan to leave France between your titre de séjour's expiration date and the date of your appointment, you can use these two documents to stay in France and get to your renewal appointment.

However, if you work or receive benefits of any kind (CAF, unemployment from Pôle Emploi), or if you plan to travel before your appointment, you should get a récipissé. A récipissé is a receipt which extends the validity of your current titre de séjour, usually by 3 months, until your appointment. Your employer may require a récipissé to prove that you still have the ability to work legally in France, and Pôle Emploi will stop your benefits at your titre de séjour's expiration date without this document. You can get a récipissé by going to the Centre de Réception des Etrangers in your préfecture with your passport, expiring titre de séjour, passport photos, convocation, and a justificatif de domicile (proof of residence.)

Going to Your Appointment.

On the day of your appointment, you should arrive before your appointment time to ensure you can get in and out as quickly as possible. If you arrive on time, you will usually wait in a long line of people who have the same appointment time as you; arriving 15-20 minutes early will ensure you receive one of the first tickets for your appointment slot.

You will have to go through a metal detector and scan your belongings before entering the préfecture, so don't bring anything dangerous or questionable with you. You can bring food and drink, and you should do so in case you have to wait a while. Most préfectures will have vending machines in the halls with coffee and snacks.

At the desk in the hall where you renew, SAY "BONJOUR", present your convocation, carte de séjour, récipissé (if you have one), and passport at the desk to receive a ticket with a number on it, and wait for your number to be called. Ensure that your documents are organized and in order, and bring change for the photocopier in case you need to make extra copies of anything. The préfecture should also have a Photomaton machine if you need to take extra photos and have €5 in cash. Get your ticket before making copies or taking photos so you have something productive you can do while you wait to be called.

They will give you a CERFA form to fill out while you are waiting with your basic information and details about your stay in France. Usually this is in A3 format so it can serve as a file folder for your documents. Fill this out in black ink and use capital letters to ensure your handwriting can be read easily.

As soon as you get to the window, SAY "BONJOUR" and present your convocation, ticket, passport, and carte de séjour / récipissé immediately. Next, present the CERFA form and the justificatif de domicile of less than 3 months. Usually the agent de guichet will then begin asking for specific documents in order. The more organized you are and the more quickly you can identify and hand over the documents, the happier everyone will be. Hand over photocopies, not originals, but have the originals handy in case they want to look. Ask if they want documents they don't ask for (but you think they might need) and let them decide whether to take them or not.

Your job is to make their job as easy as possible and to get out of there as quickly as possible. Don't chat too much, fret, or overexplain. Be polite, and answer their small talk, but recognize that they are extremely busy and have a lot of appointments to get through, so the more efficient you can be, the better. If you're potentially eligible for a multi-year card, don't be afraid to inquire about it. The agent might not offer it, but could approve you for more than one year if they're in a good mood, you're organized, and everything seems to be in order. When requesting a multi-year card, I like to write a cover letter explicitly asking for it.

Once they take your documents and ensure they have everything, they will fingerprint you and take your pictures. In the best-case scenario, they will immediately print a récipissé and affix a picture. Review it to ensure that all of your information is accurate. Note its expiration date and the status (for your ability to work) and make sure everything is spelled correctly. If everything is accurate, sign, and you're done! The agent will tell you to expect a text message to go pick up your new carte de séjour when it's ready. Don't hesitate to ask for an estimate if they don't give one.

Sometimes, after taking your documents, they pass it on to a superior for review and approval before giving you your récipissé. Don't worry, this is also completely normal. It just depends on the préfecture and their procedures. In this case, they will have you go sit down, pass on the file, and call you again once it has been approved. In the meantime, you can wait in the waiting room, usually for 45 minutes to an hour. Once you are called back, you will receive your récipissé, which you can review and sign, and then you're done.

Using Your Récipissé

You can also continue to work, travel, and receive benefits on the *renewal* récipissé you receive during your renewal appointment. The récipissé will be valid for 3 months after the appointment date.

Once you have submitted all of your documents, the préfecture will process your renewal application and produce your carte de séjour. This process takes several weeks, so you should expect to receive your carte de séjour about 2-3 months after your appointment. Sometimes, it takes longer, in which case you may want to return to the préfecture with your expiring récipissé, passport, titre de séjour, and more photos, so you can get another valid récipissé for work or benefit purposes.

Picking Up Your New Carte de Séjour

The préfecture should advise you during your appointment of how you will be notified that your carte de séjour is ready for pick-up. Usually, they will send a text message with a date and time to pick it up, although some préfectures are still sending letters by mail. You will need the text message or convocation letter to go and pick up your card.

If you do not hear anything within 10 weeks of your appointment, you should call or go to the préfecture to check your card's status. During peak times, carte de séjour renewals can take 4-5 months to be completely processed, so it's not necessarily a bad sign if your card isn't ready. And sometimes, it's merely a glitch and the text message or letter wasn't sent out. When I used to provide a self-addressed stamped envelope to receive notification for pick-up, a letter was never mailed to me and I always had to call to see if my card was ready. A client of mine never got text messages from the préfecture - until one year when she got 3 text messages in a row to say that her current renewal, along with her two previous renewals, was ready for pickup!

Once you receive notification that your card is ready, you can go to pick up your card. You will need your passport, expiring titre de séjour, récipissé (if you have one) and the amount you will have to pay in timbres fiscaux, which can be purchased online. The préfecture will tell you in your text message or letter how much you will have to pay. Be sure to ask whether they accept the timbres fiscaux purchased online, or whether you should purchase the physical stamps from a tabac. Make sure you have the correct amount in the proper format when you go.

When you arrive to pick up your carte de séjour, you will have to show your convocation if you have one (in the form of a text message or a letter) and get a ticket. Expect to wait in line a bit before you can actually receive your card. Most préfectures have a room dedicated to card pick-ups, so the process should go relatively quickly. And once you have it in hand, you can do a little dance and note the expiration date so you know when to make your next renewal appointment.

Changing Your Visa Status in France

If you are already in France with a valid visa and want to do something else, you can sometimes change your visa status without leaving the country, thereby maintaining continuity of your residence in France and ensuring the time you've already spent in France will count towards your eventual residency or naturalization application.

Changing your visa status is a long and complex process, and it is NOT easier to change your status than it is to get a certain visa type in the first place. Being in France already does not mean your application will be approved more easily. In fact, the préfecture can sometimes become suspicious of your motives for the original visa application if they think you applied for a "visitor" visa with the intention of finding work and getting a "salarié" visa, for example.

You should not take the change of status process lightly, as in extreme cases the préfecture can actually revoke your current status if they find discrepancies in your application. If you get a student visa, get PACSed or married with your partner soon after arrival, and immediately attempt to change your status, you might raise more than a few red flags. And once those red flags are flying, it will be difficult to avoid extra scrutiny on your application.

You should not expect to begin the change of status process until you have been in France for at least a year and a half, and the process will take at least several months from the time you make your initial appointment until the time your new carte de séjour with your new status arrives.

1. Ensure you can change from your current visa type to the status you want.

Not all visa types can be changed to all other visa types. I have outlined most restrictions in each visa type's individual section in this book, and you should verify that your change is possible before attempting to make the appointment. Trying to do a change of status that is not possible will only waste your time and frustrate the préfecture agents that are trying to help you. They do not have enough knowledge or experience in most cases to know what is possible, why it is possible, and whether or not you can have an exception to the rule (spoiler alert: you can't), so don't bother going around asking in six different offices if what you want to do is okay.

A few examples of what isn't possible: you can't switch from any type of work visa to a student visa. So, if you do TAPIF and then apply to a master's program, you'll have to go home to get a new visa. You can't switch to ANYTHING from salarié en mission, jeune professionnel (FACC) or work holiday (vacances travail) visas. You can't switch to anything from Long-Séjour Temporaire, or renew it. There really aren't any exceptions to these rules, unless you get married or have a French baby. (Neither of which is a strategy).

Switching from a family-type visa, like a "vie privée et familiale", to another status like profession libérale, salarié, or other work visa types, is typically allowed if you are getting un-PACSed or divorced. If this is your situation, you should write a cover letter explaining your situation, outlining your work situation and income, and specifying that you are seeking a change of status because of the impending end of your relationship. If you are salaried and do not have a 10-year card, your employer will likely have to pay the OFII tax to keep you in your position. It's better to inquire about what to do and how to do it BEFORE formally ending the relationship.

2. Renew your current visa at least once, unless you have very compelling reasons not to do so.

If you have been on your current visa type for less than one year and want to switch statuses, you are very likely to have problems, especially if your visa status is visitor or student. The préfecture can get very suspicious if it thinks that you got a visa in order to circumvent the application process for another, more difficult visa type. They will suspect that you never intended to fulfil your obligations associated with your initial visa.

Changing status from student or visitor without renewing once would be difficult, if not impossible, for example. But if you are doing the TAPIF program, which ends after 7-8 months, and want to switch to another status, it is feasible. In the latter situation, you would not be avoiding your obligations under your visa type, but instead you would simply be seeking a new status because the program that allowed you to move to France has ended.

Seek professional guidance on this topic before you attempt to change your status if you have any doubts about your ability to do so. Sometimes it is easier and more cost-effective to return to your home country and to apply for a new visa rather than to wait and change your status in France.

3. Make your appointment.

For a change of visa status, you will have to specifically request a "changement de statut" and identify both your *current* visa type and your *future* carte de séjour status (the one you want to receive.)

You will not be able to make an appointment for a change of status on the automatic online system, so you will have to call, use the email form and explain in detail what you want to do in a comments box, or go in-person to the prefecture to make your appointment. The easiest way is to go in-person and to make the appointment directly with someone in the department that treats applications and renewals for the type of status you will be applying for.

4. Submit your application.

Some préfectures, such as Bordeaux, will require you to submit a complete change-of-status application by mail that they will pre-screen before they will give you an appointment. Others just have you make an appointment by web, email, or phone, and evaluate it after you submit it in-person.

Show up to the préfecture at the appointed date and time and submit the complete application with all of the recommended documents from the list they gave you and the list I've provided here. You want to treat the change-of-status process as being just as serious, if not more serious, as applying for the visa in your home country.

5. Wait for approval and your new carte de séjour.

You will maintain your original carte de séjour status until your new status is officially approved and you receive your new card. For example, if you are switching your visa status from student to profession libérale, you will not be able to start your microentrepreneur activity until you have received a récipissé with your new "profession libérale" status. The new card will enable you to register as a microentrepreneur, whereas your student status would not. Similarly, if you switch from "visitor" to "vie privée et familiale" by marrying a French partner, you will not be able to begin working until you get a récipissé or carte de séjour that specifies your new status and your ability to work.

In most cases, the récipissé you receive at your renewal appointment will maintain your former status until you go to pick up your new card. This is to give the préfecture time to review your application properly before officially allowing you to begin work. You should refer to the récépissé you receive at your appointment, which will specify whether your status has changed and what, if any, work authorizations you have.

Occasionally, if you are setting up a business or microentreprise, the préfecture will conditionally switch your status to allow you to register your activity. You will be given another appointment 2-3 months later so that you have time to begin registering your business with the appropriate authorities, gathering your business registration documents, opening your bank account, and starting to bill clients before you return for the second appointment. During the second appointment, you will have to show proof of your business setup and invoices for any clients you've already had in order to receive final approval and your official carte de séjour with your new status.

Getting Help with Your Visa Application

Getting professional assistance to determine your visa type and to help you to create and submit a thorough application is one of the best ways to practically ensure your success. Of course, even professional guidance is not a 100% guarantee of getting your visa, but it can eliminate or reduce most of the potential issues with your application. Having assistance throughout the visa application process can also keep you on track and reduce the stress of not knowing what you should be doing and when.

All professional services Allison provides include the stipulation that if your visa application is not successful the first time, Allison will reevaluate and rework the complete application for a resubmission at no additional charge, within one year.

If you have already submitted a visa application unsuccessfully, please do yourself a favor and consult a professional before making any subsequent submissions. Reapplying after one application failure is not ideal but possible; multiple application rejections significantly lower your chances of ever getting a French visa.

What is a "Franceformation"?

In another life, my business was called Paris Unraveled. A late friend from my choir found the name, based on the idea of unraveling the mysteries of French bureaucracy and administration, and of living in Paris. While I loved the name for several years, I started to feel like I was growing out of it. For one thing, I had inquiries from people who thought I *only* worked with people moving to Paris, and I constantly had to clarify that my clients were from all over the world and moving to all different regions of France. And I began to dislike the imagery of the word "unraveled," which depicts something falling apart. While your life may unravel as you begin to transform - there's always a breakdown before a breakthrough - "unraveling" can be a scary image rather than a positive vision of the new life you'll create.

When I was revising and renaming my service packages and my business in late 2019, I also began to acknowledge that the work I was doing wasn't just providing visa support and a completed visa application. In fact, one of the main components of the service I was providing was emotional support and coaching through my client's periods of doubt that their move would happen. And my clients wanted to feel like they were supported throughout the entire process, from conception through the "fourth trimester," or the magical period after arriving in France but before they are truly established and feeling secure. My job wasn't just about providing information and delivering the finished application, it was to be a midwife to this new life and to support them on the emotional journey they sometimes weren't prepared for as we created it together.

The concept of Franceformation ties in a few different ideas. The transformation of my client's lives, in all of the most practical ways through the emotional transformation that accompanies major life changes such as an international move. In English, the word "formation" is the creation of something new, or it can represent an orderly or organized structure. In French, the word "formation" is a training or educational program, and a Franceformation encompasses a period of learning about yourself, your dreams, and your abilities, along with more broad topics like living in France, the French visa and renewal process, and various French bureaucracy and administration. It also includes learning new language skills and adapting to a new culture and way of life. Finally, a formation is also a deposit of solid rock, which represents the solid foundation we create for the projects and life goals my clients develop.

Franceformation, / fræns fɔrˈmeɪ ʃən /, n.f.:
1. The creation of one's new life in France;
2. The personal transformation one undergoes when moving to France and incubating a new life;
3. The intense period of learning about oneself, about French bureaucracy, and about French language and culture, which occurs as one prepares to move to France and adapts to a new culture;
4. A full-service and support program to nurture you from the moment you decide to move to France, through your visa application, arrival, and beyond.

Are you ready to commit to yours?

You can leverage expertise to enhance and accelerate your Franceformation journey.

Consider that your future dream life in France is a huge canvas, and right now, it is blank. Our job while working together is first to outline the image you want to paint, and then, to paint by number, filling in colors all over the canvas until the beautiful image emerges. At the moment, if you're not even sure what visa type you'll apply for, you may not be able to envision the future image at all. And yet, it's there. The life that you want to create for yourself is inside of you, and our most important task is to extract it, in all of its glory, without damaging it or telling you that for some reason, you can't have it.

Once we have played midwives to your new life goals, our next step is to nurture and protect them as they mature, and as we begin to paint inside the lines and bring the colors to life. In this stage, during the process of determining how to bring your dream to life, it's important to continually nourish it with positive energy and excitement, and to avoid naysayers and "realists" who will be "concerned" that you are wasting your time on something that may not come to fruition. You may have your own doubts during this stage, and it's important to question your doubts and fears to prevent them from taking over. Il faut cultiver son jardin — and pull the weeds as we go.

The higher your enthusiasm, your energy, and your belief in yourself, your project, and your ability to make the move, the faster we will be able to fill in the grid and bring your dream to live. We can quickly build momentum and create the outlines of your new life, but at the same time, we have to avoid moving too fast and burning out. It's a delicate balance, to build energy and momentum on one hand, while pacing ourselves on the other. If we're not careful, moving too fast, or *danser plus vite que la musique*, the first obstacle or challenge will derail your project and your belief in your ability to make it happen.

My unique Franceformation process is a holistic process to help you identify what you want to create in each area of your life, to guide you through the visa process for creating it, and to facilitate your passage through the administrative challenges that await you during the visa application procedure and upon arrival in France.

Once you have an idea of which type of immigration you'll pursue and what your goals are, we can schedule our initial free Franceformation Clarity Call, where we'll solidify your visa plans and your timeline, and set a tentative start date for our work together, along with a tentative visa application date, so we know when to make your visa appointment.

We'll discuss your overall readiness to make your move happen. A sense of "readiness" to take a big step isn't something that comes from outside of you. It is something that you create inside of you, and you do it by taking action. While sometimes my clients have concrete time constraints, like waiting for a child to graduate, or selling their house, many times, the time constraints are in their minds. During our call, we'll discuss what actual barriers there are to beginning your move process, and what barriers you've created in your mind to hold up the process.

As we begin our work together, you'll get access to my complete library of materials to prepare you for your move to France and the administrative work that awaits you upon arrival. From a moving checklist of documents to gather and things to do before you submit your visa application, to tutorials on post-arrival procedures like enrolling your kids in school, registering your business, or filing your first French tax return, you'll be accompanied along every step of your journey.

The 5 Foundations of the Franceformation system:

Throughout my years assisting people in moving to France, not only have I developed the expertise required to help them determine the right visa type for their goals and to achieve success, I've also developed a thorough understanding of the other tools and support you'll need as you move through the relocation process. Using my previous experience with many clients, I've developed useful documentation in five key areas to help you to fill in the colors of your Franceformation canvas more quickly and more vividly than you could do it on your own.

Mindset – When preparing for such a huge life changing event like an international move, your mindset is key, and questioning or reflecting on any doubts or challenges about your ability to move to France or your ability to bring your new dream life to fruition is key to ensuring your success. Cultivating your success mindset so you continue to grow personally and professionally is a lifelong journey, and I've put together a journal of questions for you to reflect on or answer for yourself to help you better develop your mindset.

Money – Figuring out and preparing for financial security throughout the move is an important part of allowing you to feel secure during the process and confident in your ability to make the move work. It's also an important aspect of the visa application, in that a certain amount of money in cash is required for each type of visa. I've created a workbook and resources for you to calculate your expected expenses during the move, money coming in and out, and how to generate extra money to put towards your moving expenses and savings, to help you create a full-color picture of your finances as you develop your moving timeline.

Professional Development — Your career may look different in France, depending on your skills, professional experience, and ability to continue working in your same field, or not. Salaries in France are lower, benefits are higher, and overall, the ability to get a sponsored work visa can vary greatly based on your experience and salary expectations. While we will determine your likely visa path before even beginning the process, you'll have access to professional development workbooks and professional guidance on developing your career options or business ideas into full-fledged projects and plans. Once you have an idea of where your skills and experience could take you in France, we'll be able to put together a coherent and compelling strategy for your professional launch and future success in France.

Language – Speaking French, or being dedicated to learning, is essential to creating a successful and fulfilling life in France. While you'll need to find other tools and resources to improve your skills, I provide vocabulary lists for our most important bureaucratic endeavors and help you to identify the gaps in your language knowledge that you'll want to address quickly.

French Admin Preparation – There are lots of small admin tasks you can do to get ready for your move to France, from collecting copies of official documents like your birth certificate and driving record, to getting insurance documents necessary for the visa application. The admin and bureaucracy tasks you need to complete before your departure are broken down into bite-sized items you can do at your own pace, with an explanation of why you need to do each task and what you'll need each document for. Once you arrive, you'll receive access to a whole new set of informative videos, the *First 100 Days in France*, to walk you through each administrative step you need to do upon arrival to set up your life. Of course, depending on your service package, some packages include all of the French administration done for you during the first 100 days, with follow-up support available.

Decluttering the life you have now and letting go of various aspects of it is key to finding peace and happiness as part of your move. It's all too easy to bring the clutter (physical and emotional) with us, then wonder why we are frustrated, stagnant, and stuck in the new place as well as the old. Usually, when clients come to me to begin their Franceformation, they have already begun the process of ungrounding and of laying the groundwork for their new life in France.

I'm Allison.

I'm a Franceformation consultant for people moving to France to help them imagine and align with their dream lives, get the right visa for creating the life they envision and navigate the French bureaucratic procedures that will enable them to achieve their goals. I work with highly motivated, creative, and heart-centered people who want to design a whole new life for themselves in France, who struggle with finding the right path for bringing their new life to life, and who would like to be fully supported as they blossom and s'épanouir into who they truly are.

What separates my service from other relocation

consultants is I ONLY work with passionate people who are immigrating independently and because of this, clients receive personalized support and unbridled enthusiasm as they take their leap of faith into a new life, whether they're retiring or taking a sabbatical, seeking employment and visa sponsorship, or creating or moving a self-employment activity to France. Because my clients are fully supported from the very beginning - from figuring out the right work opportunity and visa for them, through the labyrinth of a full year of French administration, to understanding culture shock and the rollar coaster of cultural adaptation, all the way to the finish line of their first visa renewal, they can truly flourish and thrive in their new home.

In this interview, I want to introduce myself and talk about how I started Paris Unraveled in 2011 and became a Franceformation consultant helping people to achieve their goal of moving to France. I believe immigration is getting harder just as it's becoming more critical to creating a globalized, interconnected, and more empathetic world, and I'm on a mission to help make dreams bigger and the world smaller, one Franceformation at a time.

Who are you, how long have you been in France, and how did you end up here?
After studying abroad for a year in college, I completely fell in love with Paris, and I moved back the fall after I graduated. I've been in France for over 10 years, and I started out as a student in a master's program in comparative literature in a French university. I was excited

to study directly in a French university, not only because it improved my French so much, but also because I paid a grand total of €452 for a year of tuition AND a year of student health insurance. The same master's (not a lucrative one, I might add!) would have cost me $40,000 in tuition if I'd stayed at Columbia.

As many Americans do, I spent the first two years teaching English with TAPIF to finance my studies. Initially, I wasn't sure if I intended to stay in France, and I was applying to PhD programs back in the US. Ultimately, I began a second master's degree to be able to stay in France, and I found a job working in an American accounting firm, where I learned all about expat taxes and tax treaties.

I ended up getting married to my French boyfriend, enabling me to get French residency easily. But part of what pushed me to marriage, perhaps before I was ready (I was young!), was that fear of not being "good enough" to manage to stay in France on my own, of not finding the right job or the right kind of living to enable me to live my dream. While I don't regret being married, I do think that going the relationship route impacted my confidence in my ability to navigate the job and administrative challenges for myself, and it puts pressure on the relationship. And of course, if the relationship doesn't go well (I was lucky, but know people who weren't), it can create a whole set of problems for people who want to stay in France after ending a marriage.

What I want is to give people the freedom to create their dream lives in France, whatever that may look like, and to navigate the immigration process outside of the typical confines of employment sponsorship or marriage. The truth is that I believe those paths to relocation - while they seem easier - stifle creativity, limit freedom, and ultimately suffocate those who benefit from them. In choosing entrepreneurship, and in helping my clients to be fully informed about the different immigration possibilities and develop their own professional projects and career paths, I hope to empower them to embrace the true freedom that comes from creating their dream life outside of patriarchal and capitalist immigration structures and from becoming a citizen of the world.

What gave you the idea to move to France in the first place?

My aunt, a biology professor and a researcher, spent a year in Paris when I was 6. She taught me some French and told me about Paris, and I always wanted to come here. I always knew I'd study abroad in France.

In high school, after a friend died, I wanted to leave, to travel as far as possible, and I almost considered spending my senior year of high school doing an exchange program. I didn't, but moving to France, first to study abroad for a year and then to live permanently, ended up being an important part of my grieving process. It helped me to get away from everything and get back to myself: the pleasure of discovering new places, the peace from having beautiful surroundings, and the challenge of expressing my thoughts in a new language helped to heal my brain and my heart. I needed a complete change in my life to examine what I really wanted and how I could use my gifts to impact the world.

What were your biggest challenges when moving?
When I studied abroad, I had the full support of Columbia's study abroad program and its administrators, and they were available to answer lots of questions about French administration and completed a lot of the bureaucracy stuff on our behalf. When I moved independently, I was practically drowning in all of the stuff I had to do and figure out on my own. Even though I was completely fluent in French, I felt like I was constantly missing something or figuring out something important after-the-fact.

Plus, the isolation and lack of connection were very difficult. I suffered a lot from anxiety and panic attacks, and bouts of depression. But it took me a while to figure out what was going on, because I was mostly high-functioning. I was grateful for having social media and apps like Skype to stay in touch with family and friends back home for free, because I was very lonely for the first few years.

How did you start helping people move to France?
The fact that I could study independently for so little money made me wonder why other people, especially other students, weren't taking advantage of the opportunity to study abroad on their own instead of paying an American

university program upwards of $40,000 for the same classes. Obviously, the American university programs provided a service helping with French administration and housing and all of that stuff that made things so much easier for their students, but there was no reason why highly motivated and intelligent individuals couldn't enroll directly in French universities instead, saving thousands. I thought I had made a really important discovery, and was excited to share it with people, so I started writing about how I did it and offering to guide other students through the process.

Initially, I wrote a book, which instead became a website, and then after a couple of years, I began offering services. When I started, it was hard to get information even from official French sites, and it was practically impossible to get information in English. Facebook groups didn't exist yet, and the internet forums that existed weren't super useful and didn't always have the right information. I really pioneered a lot of the accessible how-tos of French bureaucracy and a lot of people found my site that way.

As I added more information to my site, I began offering services, first to students who wanted to study independently as I had, and then to others who wanted to move independently and work as freelancers or remote workers. The appeal of helping clients to work on all kinds of different businesses and launch many different types of entrepreneurial projects was exciting, because I love coming up with new business ideas and brainstorming how to make them work.

Have you helped anyone like me before?
In the 6 years I've been helping people move to France - and 8 years since I began writing Paris Unraveled, I've made it my mission to make French bureaucracy as accessible and as easy to undestand as possible. I've helped all kinds of clients, from EU citizens needing help with specific administrative problems like converting a driver's license or registering for unemployment benefits, to students applying for degree programs so they could seek employment in France, to aspiring self-employed people and entrepreneurs who wanted to make their own mark on the world by leaning into service as they moved.

Each person's path to France is unique, and yet, my clients all share certain commonailities and dreams. They seek to radically shift their lives, and they need the tools not just to overcome the concrete barriers of bureaucracy, but to revolutionize their mindset so they can fully embrace their dream.

What do you look for in a client? How do I know if we'll be a good fit to work together?
I love working with people who dream big and who have lots of ideas and plans. They're not just looking for one job narrowly in one field where they've already worked for years, nor are they people who are "settling" for "just" taking French classes   - they're people who are open-minded about all of the possibilities and willing to trust the process.

Sometimes, clients come to me with a very strong vision of what they want their future life in France to look like, and those people are fun to work with because the strength of their belief makes our work exciting and invigorating. Other times, the only clear desire is the desire to come to France, and we work together to fill in the grid and to imagine the possibilities for the move. In the second case, the challenge can be in refusing to get bogged down in worrying about whether a particular idea will work. In clients who don't have a specific vision yet, we have to work to establish trust, so I can pull desires out of the client to weave the application, without them feeling like I'm imposing my vision for their future life, or choosing what is easiest for my work, and without triggering a belief that "it will never work." If the client develops reluctance or resistance while we're working together, it becomes very, very difficult to co-create anything.

Why should I work with you instead of someone else?
Other relocation professionals tend to work with large international companies and be very problem-oriented. Their client is the company moving its employee, and their objective is to anticipate and solve problems of bureaucracy as they arise. It can be a great approach, and it's one I've used occasionally, but it can set people up for failure.

Why? Because when you only address individual administrative and practical issues while ignoring the identity shift it takes to successfully transform your life through an international move, you risk being blindsided by your limiting beliefs or being held back by your fears.

What if I don't know exactly when I want to move to France?

A lot of times people resist setting a fixed departure date because they're waiting: waiting for the money to be there, waiting to find the right job, waiting to be 100% certain that things are going to work out. But the truth is, if you wait until the circumstances are perfect, you're probably never going to move. You have to begin taking action first.

Part of what I do is help my clients get ready to get ready. They take the first step by deciding to work with me on creating their dream, and we weave it into a vision at the same time as we're working on whatever leads their visa application. Being emotionally and psychologically ready for the challenges of an international move, combined with a career or job change, and speaking in a new language, and living in a new culture, all takes time. Committing to the move without committing to the work of getting ready to get ready is nonsensical. And some of the packages take several months to put together, anyway, meaning that you'll be doing the work of getting ready as we're working together.

If you don't have a specific start date in mind, we can begin with a nonrefundable deposit to schedule in a tentative date and to get you access to the tools and materials I use to help clients acclimate to the reality of their move. We can reevaluate your plans as the date of our first meeting to work on your application approaches, and push back the start date a bit at no additional charge, while locking in the payment plan you chose, if you're truly not ready.

How do I know I'm ready to start the process and talk to you?
Each client has her own path to being ready to begin, and her own timeline for getting ready to be ready. Some clients have been working towards the idea of a move to France for months or years, and others have just begun the process. Aligning all of the elements of the move and of your energy so you can set yourself up to thrive and find a new level of personal fulfilment in your life can take time, but it can move more quickly when you have guidance from someone who is experienced with the particular blocks and challenges you're likely to face and who can help you navigate through them with ease.

The truth is that only you can know if you're ready to make the commitment and if you're willing to invest your time, energy, and money into making your move a reality. An international move isn't cheap, but the time and frustration you save by having help frees you up to focus on your dreams and imagining the life you want to create for yourself, instead of the nitty-gritty of the mundane administration that can trip you up and create resistance to what you want.

Removing the mental blocks and resistance to your dream is just as important as, if not more important than navigating the actual bureaucratic gatekeeping. When we work together, I can hold up a mirror to help you see what's holding you back. The personal transformation that will enable you to leave behind your current life and to create a new reality for yourself is well-worth it, but it will cost you the life you currently have and test what you are willing to give up.

What if I'm not able to invest in professional assistance for my move to France?
Having your finances in order and enough money for the visa Powers That Be is a very important part of a successful visa application - unless you're applying as the family member of a French citizen and therefore don't need to prove income and financial resources for your application. So I completely understand if investing in assistance is out of the realm of possibility at the moment.

If you truly have no money, then I want you to start by reading *Foolproof French Visas* (here: https://payhip.com/b/KG0z) to get an idea of what type of visa you'll ultimately want to apply for. Once you have a general idea of what kind of visa you'll go for and its requirements, you'll know approximately how much money you'll need to begin saving, and you can set a monthly savings goal to begin working towards your move. You can also research the amount of money you'll need for specific moving expenses, like a plane ticket from your location to

France at the time of year you'll want to move, and the average cost of a small studio apartment in the area where you want to live.

You can begin saving for your move and working on envisioning exactly what you'd like to do in France. Once the move is in the realm of financial possibility, it will be easier to align you with an employment opportunity and a visa type and to determine how you specifically may benefit from personalized assistance. When you move closer to your goal, the path will become clearer.

If you have some financial resources and are questioning your readiness, I want you to carefully consider whether you're holding back on the investment because you're afraid that the move won't work out, and ask yourself a few questions:
- Are you not committing financially to your Franceformation because you're worried about paying for something that might not work out?
- Are you holding on to the money because you're worried that you might not get more quickly enough, and then you might not have enough for the visa application and relocation expenses themselves?
- Do you feel like you have to struggle and do everything yourself to fully "deserve" this major life change? Do you feel like it's somehow cheating or making it too easy to have someone guiding you through the process?
- Are there other areas in your life, or is it a pattern for

you, that you won't fully commit until the results are guaranteed and you know exactly how things are going to turn out?

It's okay if you're not ready. And it's okay if you're getting ready to be ready. Financial constraints can be very real, but if you're going to commit to completely changing your life, you owe it to yourself. Let it take as long as it takes, but denying yourself the support you'll need to ensure your success is only going to prolong the struggle.

Franceformation Client Case Studies

Jasmine, photographer with a profession libérale visa

My client Jasmine came to me after an immigration lawyer screwed up her case.

She had been in France for several years, and was a photographer - a hugely talented photographer, at that. She had been in France on several different visas from the Long Stay Visitor visa she'd gotten when she'd PACSed her French partner, to the vie privée after they'd been living together for more than a year, then back to Visitor after they'd broken up.

An immigration lawyer had helped her to put together an application for a change of status in Paris, and then, when that failed, a new "profession liberale" visa application in the US, but both were turned down.

Why? Two reasons.

One: she was unsure of being able to make enough money for the PL visa by doing just one type of photography, so she wrote a business plan including *every* type of photography she was capable of doing - from weddings and portraits to real estate listings to tourist photo shoots. Her business plan was unfocused, and a skeleton of what it should have been. (The lawyer, to whom she had paid an obscene sum of money, just collected the documents, but didn't help with actually writing the documents.)

To make matters worse, the wording on her website suggested that she was *already* working in Paris (she wasn't - she had just prepared her website as part of creating her business idea), on the Visitor visa, even though she technically didn't have the right to be working.

(In the game of French bureaucracy, you only need one strike to be out, and that was two.)

We began working together by renewing her existing visa and developing a plan for her change of status. I explained the problems with her previous application and asked her what she wanted to focus on - and we discussed strategies for ensuring the Préfecture wouldn't get the wrong idea.

I helped her to renew her visitor visa, so she could apply for a change of status directly in France, without going back to the US *again*, and then, we got to work on her business plan.

We niched down her business, focusing on her main skill sets and the type of photography she REALLY wanted to be doing. We got her letters of support from friends, previous clients, and a few potential clients who wanted to hire her for their ongoing photography needs. We set her rates and projected her finances.

It was a long, drawn out process, especially since the prefecture requested more information about her marketing strategies and business structure after we submitted her dossier, as DIRECCTE thought it looked like she was starting a photography studio - requiring more money and more equipment - and wanted to be sure that she could pay her business expenses. (She's actually an autoentrepreneur).

It took over a year before she FINALLY got her carte de séjour, but now, Jasmine is doing an AMAZING job, photographing events all over the city, and traveling to other parts of France. Her photography is featured regularly in several France-based magazines, she has had her work featured in international publications such as Buzzfeed, and she works consistently for some of the major organizations serving Americans in France.

Lola, tour guide in Paris with a profession libérale visa

Today, I want to tell you about my client and friend Lola, who came to France in July 2017.

Lola wanted to come to France ever since she spent her spring semester studying abroad in Paris, and just knew she had to come back. In that way, she was a lot like me - I spent my whole second semester of my junior year in Paris planning how I would return as soon as possible. I even debated not leaving!

But Lola, who's Canadian, had lived in the US, and Singapore, and all over the world, and she was working in an art history museum in the US when she found me.

Now, the thing I love about Lola is that she totally claims to have "manifested" me.

Having seen the movie The Secret about attracting what you want into your life, Lola had taken steps towards manifesting her move to Paris LONG before she figured out how she was going to make it happen.

She just didn't know how it was possible.

She had Paris-themed deco in her bathroom.

A "Take me to Paris!" button on her winter coat.

She KNEW with every fibre of her being that she was making the move. The question was, when?
She began researching. And she stumbled across Paris Unraveled.

We set up a call, and she told me about how she LOVED her museum job, had majored in art history in college, and how her favourite part of studying in Paris was the Museum Studies class - where she had gotten to go to a different museum every class period, three times a week, and learn EVERYTHING about Paris art and history.

I asked her if she had ever thought about becoming a tour guide, and explained that she could get a "profession liberale" visa to work as a freelance tour guide for multiple companies in Paris, who are always enthusiastic about hiring autoentrepreneur tour guides with art history degrees.

She'd have no trouble finding work with one or more of these companies, I explained, and she could even create her own tour experiences on platforms like AirBnb Experiences or her own website.

And BOOM, just like that. Lola had her "how."

Over about 2 months, I helped Lola put together her business plan for her profession liberal visa application, drawing on her museum experience, love of Paris and all things art history, and her university studies to create a fan-freaking-tastic visa application package.

Today, Lola is a thriving tour guide in Paris, living on l'Ile Saint-Louis and working for 3 tour companies, making BANK during tourist season, and traveling to all kinds of fantastic places - from champagne producers near Reims, to the Normandy beaches and the Mont Saint Michel, to walking tours of Montmartre and the Eiffel Tower.

She renewed her initial visa in the fall of 2018 and she is well on her way to French residency, and as long as she continues her success, she'll be able to live and work in

France indefinitely.

Jordan, English coach with a change of status from student to profession libérale

My client Jordan came to France as a student, studying French and photography. Having completed a TEFL certification, she soon found a part-time job teaching English, and then, hit what I'd call the student job jackpot.

A tech startup wanted to hire her to develop their English curriculum, evaluate the English level of their employees, and provide lessons. It wasn't just "teaching English," it was "English coaching."

To comply with her student visa, they offered several different solutions. She worked for a while through a "portage salarial," an independent company that registers you as an employee and pays full social charges on your behalf. It cost 50% of her total gross income - but the company was willing to pay.

Then, they hired her on a part-time CDI, and she was able to work about 20h per week on her student visa, around her language classes.

As her time as a student drew to an end, and her photography classes finished, she wondered what the next step was. The job wasn't able to sponsor her, but would be willing to keep her. She wasn't going to remain a student for much longer, but didn't want to leave. We decided to put together a profession liberal visa application so she wouldn't be "just" an English teacher, but an English coach, using her skills with startup companies who wanted to develop their markets abroad, and providing professional English lessons related to their fields. It would enable her to continue working for her current company, switching from a CDD position to a contractor position after her contract expired, and to work with other tech companies and independent professionals who wanted to use English in a professional setting - and who wanted their company to pay for their skills.

Over the course of a few weeks, we calculated an appropriate hourly coaching rate for continuing with her current company, and put together service packages to pitch to other companies, leveraging her skills evaluating employees' English to determine their learning needs, as well as putting together individualised learning plans and coaching packages to attain those skills. Her current company signed a contract for ongoing professional services, and she began approaching other, similar companies who might benefit from offering the same service to their employees.

After she successfully submitted her visa application at the Paris prefecture, we set up her business, and she began marketing her services to independent clients as well, and quickly began selling packages of multiple tutoring and coaching sessions to complement her income from the one main client. She has plans to turn her coaching skills into short online programs touching on several important English skills for professionals, like professional small talk and professional communication and email writing in English.

Her first carte de séjour is up for renewal this summer, and there's no doubt in my mind she'll get multiple years due to her rapid success in launching her business and transforming her clients' careers.

Anna, web designer with a profession libérale visa

My client Anna registered for the Complete French Business Incubator during the summer of 2018. An avid traveler, she had developed skills in web design and development, and wanted to move to France and start her own web design business.

She already worked with a few clients in the US, but didn't have standardised packages, or a summary of what services she could provide on an ongoing basis. She had some friends in France, but didn't have any clients here yet - something she felt was crucial if she wanted to start a successful business here.

Anna already had an idea of what she wanted to charge for her services, and took advantage of our individual calls and FrancoFiles office hours to discuss research into market rates in France and the US for the services she wanted to offer, which we researched together.

We identified the types of clients she wanted to work with, and what her ideal clients needed most from an independent web developer. Then, I helped her go from outlining various services she could perform for them at an hourly rate, to identifying which services could be sold together as a package, and how many hours each service would take. Then, we used the information about her ideal clients' needs to craft several sample packages and put together several sample proposals of what she could offer a small business owner. Not all of her clients would have the same needs, and her packages and quotes would be customised for each individual client, but she had a jumping-off point for what she could show the prefecture and a prediction for what the potential income from different projects could be. Using the Business Blueprint and Business Plan Sections Workbooks from the Complete French Business Incubator, Anna put together an a-freaking-mazing 40 page business page for her activity, including the sample proposals we created, an analysis of other small web design businesses in the market, and her income projections, and submitted a very thorough profession liberal visa application to the VFS office in Chicago, not long after the visa submission process had changed. (Of course, VFS had no clue what visa type she was applying for or what documents she needed - but fortunately, she knew!)

One problem arose as she waited for her passport to be returned with her visa. She had referred to the business not by her own name, but by a "Studio" name. Because her business looked SO GOOD on paper, the consulate mistook her business for being *much larger* than she intended. A few weeks after she submitted her project (longer than it usually takes for my clients to get their visas back), the consulate sent her an additional form to fill out, about the space she was leasing, her investments, and the employees she was hiring! They had assumed, based on her level of detail and income, she was applying for a "passport talents" visa and submitted her application to DIRECCTE to evaluate the plan - something that only happens for brick-and-morter businesses or businesses requiring large investments.

We jumped on a call and I explained the misunderstanding, and together, we completed the form and wrote an additional letter to the consulate to clarify her business and status as an independent / auto entrepreneur, and to explain that she would be working from her laptop by herself, without any employees.
She FINALLY got her visa nearly 13 weeks after she submitted her application, and arrived in France soon after, ready to set up shop. I'm happy to report that she is now successfully running her web design business with clients from all over the world.

Claire, Pilates instructor and personal trainer with a profession libérale visa

Today, I want to tell you about my client Claire, and how I helped her move *back* to France and start her own business.

Claire, a Canadian, had lived in France before for a short time after doing a degree program in Scotland, but had returned to the US to work as a Pilates instructor and physical therapist. After a time, she discovered that she REALLY wanted to come back to France, but wasn't sure how to make it work.

When we talked on the phone, I told her that her qualifications from the UK would be valid in France, but that there would be a process to get them recognised. However, she could apply for a profession libérale visa as a Pilates instructor, and then work on getting her credentials recognised so she can also practice as a kinésithérapeute.

Claire had plenty of friends, acquaintances, and past clients from her previous France life who were willing to sign letters of support and letters stating that they were eager to begin working with her as an English speaking Pilates clients to improve their health and fitness once she was able to begin working in France.
She had already developed her packages and knew her rates.

We put together a business plan that identified a couple of important target markets for her services:
expat moms who wanted to begin a fitness regime in a small group class. Business travelers and tourists who wanted to continue their exercise regime while vacationing

in Paris by doing something fun, like Pilates in the park. Then, we worked on outlining how her services would work: how she would market and find clients, how she would evaluate them and put together an exercise plan based on their individual needs, and how she would sell her packages and services.

We talked about where she could host client sessions where she'd be able to use Pilates equipment - too expensive for her to buy on her own - and how she'd have to get professional insurance and an 'éducateur sportive' card. Now, she's in France, and we're in the process of filing her kinésithérapeutie application and doing all of her business and professional registrations, so she is able to work with clients and be legally insured and covered for the type of work she does.

Did You Know?

95% of Paris Unraveled clients who have used the Complete French Business Incubator program since 2017 have successfully obtained profession libérale or profession artistique visas.

98% of Paris Unraveled clients who have submitted a visa application prepared by Paris Unraveled have successfully obtained their visa.

Since 2013, Allison & Paris Unraveled has provided visa application preparation services for over 50 people, and has helped hundreds of clients with French admin questions and assistance.

Between the FrancoFiles community, Virtual Office Hours, and the Americans in France Facebook group, Allison has answered over 30,000 questions about French bureaucracy and administration.

Since becoming an admin of the Americans in France group in 2013, Allison has grown the group from under 700 members to over 11,000 members in 2020. Allison's Americans in France group is widely recognized in the expat community as *THE* go-to place to get questions answered about French admin or to discuss French culture.

Client Testimonials

Allison is an expert guide through the intricacies and difficulties of french bureaucracy. Not only is she deeply knowledgeable, she is also kind and funny. She makes you feel like you have a friend and ally, which makes the whole process feel infinitely less stressful. Thanks again for a great chat! Alexa

You were very helpful in the short time we spoke, I wanted to know if I had to get a long stay visa to come to France and get married and you answered that question easily. You put my mind at ease about my move to France, I thought it would involve traveling to Los Angeles first to obtain a long stay Visa in order to get married in France. Michael Benton

Great to meet you and this was a perfect introduction to your services. As I've been toying around in my head with this idea for about 10 years, it feels good to make a proactive step and to know that there is a resource I can reach out to when it all starts to get REAL. Hopefully in the next few months I will have a more decided timeline and can determine which package will make most sense. You are totally the missing puzzle piece! You can use my first name for sure. Though I'm not sure I've said anything very quotable yet. - Jane

I have been reading some articles Paris Unraveled since I moved to Paris two years ago. I am an older artist with long term visitors visa so I can't work. I contacted Allison to ask for consultation and it was great that she gave me thirty minutes of her time explaining through my options very cleary and comprehensively. Now I have few options to consider and a good idea about how to go about changing my visa status. Allison is well informed and extremely knowledgeable and I would greatly recommend her service. Sophia H.

"Paris Unraveled answered my email within a few hours and Allison immediately set up a call with us to go over our questions. My wife and I are well traveled and experienced in navigating foreign countries and initially thought we could do this on our own, no problem. After speaking with Allison we quickly discovered some of our basic assumptions were wrong and she provided extensive information to assist us in our planned move to Paris. Its clear she knows here stuff here and we look forward to her guiding us on our Parisian Journey from the States." - Anthony, New York City

The call helped me understand the visa options available to me and out of those which is probably the best for me, what is required and how long it could take. I learned about various visa related issues I was not aware of. It was extremely helpful. Thank you so much. - Simon

Anyone considering a move to France should strongly consider using Allison. She has an incredible wealth of knowledge, someone I would consider to be a subject matter expert. She lays out the groundwork and steps in an extremely efficient manner. Please do not consider a move to France without first consulting with her. - Mark

Before I met Allison I thought the visa process to studying French in France would be lengthy and full of headaches. Allison made it a swift and smooth process. In just 1 meeting we had everything together and ready to send. 1 month later I got to France and started studying! Allison is wonderful and École l'étoile is truly a dream. Thank you so much Allison! - Bobby

I'm an American artist who moved to France last year, and don't know what I would have done without Allison. I had no idea how challenging things would be once I arrived in France especially the bureaucracy. Allison has been extremely helpful and professional, by going above and beyond to help me with my visa as well as helping me with setting up my business to run in France. If you need help with anything in France, Allison is the person to ask! - Kimbra

Excellent, very clear that Allison knew what she was talking about and had plenty of experience. If only we could go back in time to our arrival in France and use Allison from the start! - Jason

"The session with Allison was worth every cent, and has put my mind at ease. The French tax system is complicated, and Allison's deep knowledge of the system and the things that can trip expats up proved invaluable.

She was also able to explain things in a clear way so that I understood the concepts and different types of taxation. I feel calmer knowing that Allison is there and that I can return to her if I have any future queries. I just couldn't work it all out for myself, no matter how much research I did - so was very grateful to tap into everything Allison has learnt over the years." - Naomi

Allison is highly knowledgeable and informed on current requirements, explains concepts beautifully, and is very easy to talk with. Our 45-minute session inspired the critical trust and confidence I need to have when working with a professional on such an important process and I am very much looking forward to working with her to assist with the complexities of my upcoming relocation. - Simone

"Allison has an encyclopedic knowledge of the ins and outs of the famously formidable French bureaucracy, plus a good sense of how best to approach it. Particularly useful are her alerts about the "unknown unknowns"—the requirements that we not only did not know how meet, but were unaware of in the first place. She's the person you have looking for if you are looking for a helpful, capable person to hold your hand as you settle in to life in France."
— Steve

Schedule a Consultation

Allison offers two types of individual consultations aside from visa application preparation services and Franceformation packages.

Franceformation Clarity Calls

A Franceformation Clarity Call is a free 45-minute call to help you come to a decision about how and when to move forward on your planned move to France. During this call, you introduce yourself, your plans, and your timeline, and we discuss the best visa options to fit your unique situation. Then, when we've gotten to know each other, we'll discuss the options for working together on your visa application and relocation to see if it's a good fit.

Request a Franceformation Clarity Call if you're ready to begin the process of moving (or renewing your visa, changing your status, or another specific administrative need) and would like to see whether getting assistance with the process is the right fit for you.

Complete a request here to schedule a call: https://www.yourfranceformation.com/packages/

Individual Franceformation Consultations

Early in the exploratory stage of your planning process, you may not yet ready to commit to working on a visa application, and you may still have questions you'd like answered about how everything works in France. You may just want to talk through your options, the tax implications, the administrative procedures, and more before you make any hard decisions about whether moving is right for you and which direction you'll go with your visa application.

If you're contemplating a move but have a million questions before you're ready to make a decision, you can schedule a one-hour paid consultation to get your questions answered. If you then enroll as a Franceformation client within 6 months, the cost of your paid consultation will be deducted from the fee for the services you choose.

Schedule a paid call: https://payhip.com/b/qMDs

Also by Allison Lounes

The 5 Decisions Big Dreamers Make Before Their Franceformation

is a newly-released aspirational book to help you determine whether you're ready to take the leap and move to France, and, if you're not yet ready, to show you how to get there. After working with dozens of clients who successfully and enthusiastically made the transition to living in France - and a handful of former clients who ultimately gave up pursuing their dream, Allison has identified the qualities most commonly embodied by the people who seem to effortlessly rise to the challenge of pursuing their international move. What makes them different, and how do they think differently about themselves and about their move? And are there beliefs or behaviors you can embrace in your own life to help you get ready to get ready to Franceform?

Link to purchase: https://payhip.com/b/5SRi

Made in the USA
Monee, IL
01 October 2020